SAMUEL SELVON

SAMUEL SELVON

Roydon Salick

NORTHCOTE
BRITISH COUNCIL

1006904683

© Copyright 2013 by Roydon Salick

First published in 2013 by Northcote House Publishers Ltd, Horndon, Tavistock, Devon, PL19 9NQ, United Kingdom.
Tel: +44 (01822) 810066. Fax: +44 (01822) 810034.

British Library Cataloguing-in-Publication Data
A catalogue record for this book is available from the British Library

ISBN 978-0-7463-1089-2 hardcover
ISBN 978-0-7463-0974-2 paperback

Typeset by TW Typesetting, Plymouth, Devon
Printed and bound in the United Kingdom

For Nalini

Contents

Acknowledgements

I would like to thank Mr Ernest Joseph and Mrs Arlene Dolabaille of UWI Library, St Augustine, Trinidad, for their help in sourcing Selvon's poems and short stories. Ken Ramchand, as always, has been generous with his books, comments, and encouragement. Shelley Persaud, Selvon's daughter from his first marriage, Hazeljoy Harrison, Selvon's niece, and Gerald Boodhram, Selvon's nephew, have provided welcome biographical information and pictures. Mr Vaughn Jardine, LAN Administrator, Campus IT Services, UWI, St Augustine, has assisted with computer problems. My greatest debt is to my wife, to whom this volume is dedicated.

Biographical Outline

1923   Samuel Dickson Selvon is born on 20 May at 42 Mount Moriah, San Fernando, the southern city in Trinidad, to Daisy (half-Scottish, half-Indian) and Bertwin Selvon (Madrasi).

1928   Selvon enters Vistabella CMI School (now Vistabella Presbyterian).

1929   Selvon transfers to San Fernando CMI School (now known as Grant Memorial Presbyterian).

1934   Selvon enters Naparima College, a secondary school in San Fernando for boys founded in 1900 and run by Canadian Missionaries.

1939   Selvon leaves Naparima College, without securing the Cambridge School Certificate. Here, his compositions are praised by his English teacher, Rev. Walls, who encourages him to keep writing. Selvon works at the Pointe-a-Pierre Oil Refinery as an accounts clerk.

1940–5 Selvon joins the Royal Navy Reserve, working as a wireless operator on various navy ships.

1941   Selvon meets Ismith Khan for the first time at the wedding of Dennis Selvon (Sam's older brother) and Betty Khan (Ismith's older sister). The lifelong friendship between the two writers had significant implications for the literature of Trinidad and Tobago and for West Indian literature.

1946–9 Selvon joins the staff of the *Trinidad Guardian*, in which newspaper, he publishes his first poems, short stories and non-fiction pieces. His work brings him into contact with such aspiring writers as Lamming, Errol Hill and Clifford Roach, among others.

1947   Selvon marries Draupadi Persaud, and moves to Barataria, the village to which Tiger and Urmilla migrate in *A Brighter Sun*. The Selvons leave Mount Moriah in 1948 to join their son in Barataria. They live long enough to share in the success of *ABS*; they die within months of each other in 1953 and 1954.

1950   Selvon emigrates to England.

1951–4   Selvon works at menial jobs, and secures employment as a clerk in the Indian Embassy in London.

1952   *A Brighter Sun* is published. Selvon contracts tuberculosis and spends a little more than a year in hospital. While at hospital Selvon decides to become a full-time writer.

1954   Selvon is released from hospital. He is awarded a Guggenheim Fellowship.

1955   *An Island is a World*, the first of two middle-class novels, is published.

1956   *The Lonely Londoners*, the first novel of the Moses trilogy, is published.

1957   *Ways of Sunlight*, Selvon's first collection of short stories, is published.

1958   *Turn Again Tiger*, a sequel to *A Brighter Sun*, is published.

1963   *I Hear Thunder*, the second middle-class novel, is published. Selvon marries Althea Deroux.

1965   *The Housing Lark*, Selvon's second immigrant novel, is published.

1969   Selvon, paid by Tate & Lyle to write a book on the local sugar industry, spends his longest return visit at Tacarigua, where he completes *The Plains of Caroni*. Selvon is awarded the Humming Bird Medal by the Trinidad & Tobago government.

1970   *The Plains of Caroni*, the third peasant novel, is published.

1972   *Those Who Eat the Cascadura*, Selvon's final peasant novel, is published. Draupadi Persaud dies of cancer in her native Guyana.

1975   *Moses Ascending*, a sequel to *The Lonely Londoners*, is published. Selvon is appointed Fellow in Creative Writing at the University of Dundee.

1978	Selvon migrates to Calgary, Canada.
1982	Selvon is appointed the first Writer in Residence at UWI, St Augustine, Trinidad.
1983	*Moses Migrating*, the final narrative of the Moses trilogy, is published.
1985	Selvon is appointed Writer in Residence at the University of Winnipeg, Manitoba, Canada. Selvon is awarded an LLD from UWI.
1988	*El Dorado West One*, a seven-part radio drama, is published.
1989	*Foreday Morning*, a selection of Selvon's prose writings, is published. Selvon is awarded an LLD from the University of Warwick.
1991	*Highway in the Sun*, a collection of four radio dramas, is published.
1994	On his last visit to Trinidad, Selvon, while playing scrabble, suffers a massive heart attack. He is hospitalized, and a month or so later, dies on 16 April. He is buried in the UWI cemetery, St Augustine, Trinidad.

Abbreviations

The following abbreviations are used in the text and notes of this book.

ABS	*A Brighter Sun*
EDWO	*El Dorado West One*
FM	*Foreday Morning*
HL	*The Housing Lark*
HS	*Highway in the Sun* (the volume of radio dramas)
HSRD	*Highway in the Sun* (the radio drama)
HW	*Harvest in Wilderness*
ISH	*India Sweet Home*
IHT	*I Hear Thunder*
IW	*An Island is a World*
LL	*The Lonely Londoners*
MA	*Moses Ascending*
MM	*Moses Migrating*
POC	*The Plains of Caroni*
SC	The Selvon Collection (manuscript material donated by Selvon to the University of the West Indies, St Augustine, Trinidad in 1987).
TAT	*Turn Again Tiger*
TATRD	*Turn Again Tiger* (the radio drama)
TWEC	*Those Who Eat the Cascadura*
WS	*Ways of Sunlight*

Introduction

Much of the criticism of Selvon's works over the last four decades has focused on the novels, especially the immigrant novels. Except for two introductions (Ramchand, Grant), an article by Wyke, and scattered comments, there is little of value on the short fiction; Nasta's introduction to *El Dorado West One* is still the only critical essay on the radio dramas, and Ramchand's article on Selvon's 'love songs' remains the solitary critique of the poems. Although there are numerous articles on the novels, and several discussions of Selvon in composite studies (Forbes, Procter, Sandhu, Dawson, Joseph, Ball, among others), there are to date only four book-length studies (Wyke, 1991; Looker, 1996; Salick, 2001; Sindoni, 2006); these deal exclusively with his novels. There is in these four studies the occasional reference to specific short stories but no mention whatsoever of the poems or the radio dramas; indeed, from these books, the reader comes away with the delusive notion that Selvon wrote ten novels and a few short stories. Though the longer narratives are the works upon which his reputation as one of the most important West Indian authors rests, critics can no longer afford to disregard his other categories of writing. The protracted critical neglect of the poems, radio dramas and the short fiction continues to impoverish our understanding of Selvon's artistic versatility. The poems are the most personal pieces in the corpus and reveal a private side of Selvon discovered nowhere else. The radio dramas show Selvon's grasp of the demands of a new and challenging genre with which he felt comfortable. The short fictional pieces are many and uneven in quality; there are, however, dozens of truly splendid short stories and

1

ballads. This study consciously bucks the critical trend in a sanguine attempt to correct the mistaken impression that Selvon is purely a novelist; it is the first sustained analysis of all the facets of Selvon's fictional world: the poems, radio dramas, short fiction, and the novels.

The published radio dramas, adaptations of five novels, form an unfamiliar but unique category; they borrow liberally from the novels, changing the nature and chronology of events, ultimately transforming the novels into dramatic works that are quite different from the originals. The adapting from one medium to another makes it impossible to discuss the dramas without reference to the novels; this accounts for both the weaknesses and the strengths of the dramas. In these adaptations, there is an unmistakable preference for the comic incident and situation; for example, the narrative of *Turn Again Tiger*, Selvon's second peasant novel, becomes a dramatic comedy, whose focus is the love relationship between Otto and Berta. In one extreme case, the novel, *An Island is a World*, is unrecognizable in the radio-drama adaptation, *Home Sweet India*. All that is crucial to understanding why Selvon considered this his most important novel is lost. In his radio dramas Selvon exploited the immigrants' need to connect with their Caribbean island homes through hearing their language spoken and through the highlighting of incidents and behaviour peculiar to their culture. These dramas (and two television plays) would also have brought an habitually impecunious Selvon much-needed funds.

The poems are among the earliest pieces Selvon published; these juvenile pieces are quite variable. Some are banal, others reveal the young writer's need to wrestle with existentialist issues, quite a few address the many sides of the love experience, a handful focus on the need for proper perspective in the interest of forming a balanced assessment of an experience, some deal with the changeful nature of the tropical landscape and the most difficult deal with aspects of the creative process. Those that are neither substantial nor memorable deal with lost love; those that are sincere and moving deal with love that is vibrant and assuring and with the exploration of ponderable themes. Whatever our opinion of the poems, we cannot deny that they are crucial in any assessment of Selvon, the artist. Their significance lies in their revelation of the concerns that exercised the mind of the fledging writer, emphasizing an existentialist outlook on life, love and experience. Mutability, the fear that life does not provide what is needed to understand it, the topsy-turvy experience of love, and the difficulty of adequately expressing experience in art are predominant themes.

The short stories are many and fall into four categories: urban stories that depict the Afro-Trinidadian working-class world, rural stories about the Indo-Trinidadian peasant experience, London-based stories that deal with the problems of immigrant life of an almost exclusively Afro-West Indian community (only one ballad 'Knock on Wood' centres around an Indo-Trinidadian character), and stories that focus on the creative process. They present wide-ranging themes not found in the poems. Selvon, the storyteller, is more at home in these narratives than in the poems: he has more to say, and he says it well. Selvon explores the inevitable tension between Hindu custom and Creole culture; interrogates Hindu tradition that is represented as retardative; approves the wisdom of becoming creolized in a plural society; advocates the need for mutual respect among the ethnic groups; highlights the relationship between folklore and the human mind; establishes the value of industry and perseverance; endorses a heroism that defines the struggle of both individual and community; posits the value of humour to the West Indian island-dweller and immigrant; and investigates the role of the creative imagination.

Such defining themes, and more, expectedly, are reprised in the ten novels, three of which have their beginning in a short story (the relationship between the novels and the short stories is investigated at length in the chapter on Selvon's short fiction). The novels are easily the most important versions of the narratives, expanding the respective short stories by broadening thematic concerns, widening the geographical setting, deepening characterization, and complexifying narrative techniques. They fall into three separate categories: peasant novels, middle-class novels and immigrant novels. Taken together they paint the largest, most detailed canvas in West Indian literature of Trinidadians at work and play over four decades, from the declaration of the Second World War to the post-independence experience in the 1960s and 1970s. The peasant novels fictionalize the tremendous struggle Indo-Trinidadian peasants experienced over a century to assume their well-deserved place in all walks of island life, even winning the highest political office on two occasions. The middle-class novels present both sides of the bourgeois picture, emphasizing the significant contributions of committed, thinking professionals (*An Island is a World*), as well as recognizing the indifference of those too self-centered and superficial to care (*I Hear Thunder*). The immigrant novels exchange the genial, colourful island setting for the foggy ambivalence of 'the great city' of London, to which Selvon emigrated in 1950. These novels chronicle the fleeting summer pleasures, the anxious winter struggle, and the loneliness of being children of the empire, marginalized, rejected and humiliated by the motherland.

The composition and contents of this revisionist volume make it unique among all critical writings on Selvon; it renders encyclopedia entries and such compilation essays as Fabre's (1979, 1995) outdated and misleading. Its definitive merit is that it presents in one continuous context critical assessments of all aspects of Selvon's artistic output. The reader leaves it not only with the knowledge that Selvon wrote poems, radio dramas, short fiction and novels, but also with an understanding of how each fictional category works autonomously and how each participates in the creation of a comprehensive portrait of Selvon, the writer. It is, therefore, the first balanced and complete introduction to the Selvon corpus, inviting readers to make inter-modal linkages, generic cross-references and comparisons, in the interest of arriving at a more just and rewarding estimate of Selvon's *oeuvre* and achievement. This study encourages continuing interest in the novels, especially the peasant and middle-class novels, on which much remains to be written; more importantly and urgently, it underscores the need for greater critical attention to be devoted to the less familiar categories – poems, dramas and short fiction. If it does only that, it would happily have served its express purpose; in time, the perception of Selvon as predominantly a novelist will metamorphose into the acceptance of Selvon as one of the most versatile of West Indian writers.

1

The Poems

Selvon's poems (1946–73) fall into four clear categories: love poems, nature poems, existentialist poems and poems that deal with the world of art.[1] These categories, however, are not discrete: in a few of the love poems and art poems there is existentialist thought, and in several nature poems there is a concern with the creative process. Moreover, there are at least two positive poems ('Wings of Thought' and 'Consolation') which do not easily fit into any category. The categories suggest a wide range of themes: the puzzlement and hurt of lost love, the fullness of marital contentment, the joy of being in love, pride in celebrating the beauty of the island's changeful landscape, the marginalization and depreciation of the artist by a philistine society, the opacity of modern art, the unease of mutability, tentative hope that there are second chances, the irreparable loss of innocence and the glory of youth, and frightening facets of the existentialist experience. Such themes and more are the chosen threads Selvon weaves together to produce an engaging but dark poetic tapestry; though there is the occasional splash of deep yellow and scarlet, there is a predominance of shades of grey under a leaden sky.

Several of the love poems deal with the condition of the forlorn male lover, perplexed by the vagaries of love; Selvon many times found himself in such a situation. A very attractive man, physically and socially, and irresistible to many of the island's nubile women, he was no philanderer; he fell deeply in and out of love. Lost love, therefore, was an experience to which he was used and which he tried to understand as lover and poet; writing poems on lost love therefore is as much

5

exorcism as it is therapy. 'The Empty Glass', the first published poem, describes the mutability of the love experience: the lover has gone much too soon taking with her the loving cup, the symbol of their love, and leaving in its place a 'love-empty glass, [and] bitter-filled vessel', the symbol of the vacuity he now experiences. The unappeased loss of love has made him a vagabond, 'wandering in the mist' and wondering, too, about the dramatic change in his fortunes; unable to come to terms with the vicissitudes of love, the speaker resignedly raises his empty glass in a bravado toast, grateful for the 'little love' that his life has known. In 'Love Gone' the situation is somewhat different: although the male speaker does not know why his love has gone, he accepts the fact that she 'has fled the past'. The 'last parting' occurs in an atmospheric ambience that is right for romance ('first April shower', 'a little after gloaming time' and a 'drizzle [that] [h]aloed the lights about'); this no doubt deepens the speaker's incomprehension of her reason for leaving, underscored by the triple repetition of 'I shall never know'. In 'Grave-Digger', moreover, the gnawing loss of love transforms the speaker into a ghoulish figure desperately driven, even in the sunshine, to disinter a dead, rotting, or skeletal love; he has not achieved the closure necessary for moving on. The turnabout in his emotional fortunes is reflected in the change in the setting: the 'past' initially a landscape of hill, valley and distant shore, has become, because of the lover's '[c]old and cruel heart' a desecrated cemetery, in which a grave will be opened and robbed. 'Come Back' presents a more challenging dramatic situation: after a three-year separation, evidently by her design, the lovers meet one morning; the combination of being with his ex-lover and the sunny morning affects him sufficiently to cause the 'queer' thought of resuming the relationship. The 'queer thought', however, is merely fleeting: although the lovers reunite briefly, there is really no meaningful 'come back' (response, return). Unlike at the end of 'Grave-Digger', the speaker appears to accept that the love is no more.

Different from the love poems discussed above, are 'Petranella' and 'I Vow Madness' Selvon's second and third poems; both are closely related, being romantic hyperboles in which the speaker pedestals the loved one. In the former,

Petranella represents the idea of being in love; the enunciation of the four magic syllables of the name activates and substantiates the cosmos for the speaker. Petranella is muse-like in that she elicits from the poet the melody of words; she is the demiurgic word that sets in motion the functions of the universe. The intrinsic relationship between love and poetry is a primary theme in Selvon's poetry: life and love are essentially poetry, and poetry cannot exist without love. In 'I Vow Madness' the idea of love is incarnated, almost as if Petranella comes down to earth in human form, too beautiful in 'the morning sun' or in '[m]oonlight' standing and staring at the 'ravish[ed]' speaker. No longer ethereal, her beauty is nevertheless beyond hope and words.

Standing alone among the love poems is 'Life With You', Selvon's simplest and finest love poem, dedicated to his first wife, Droupadi.[2] Discrete from the poems about lost love and those in which the lover is pedestalled, this poem is grounded in reality as it celebrates the humility, sincerity and fullness of love in its freshness. The speaker likens himself to a seafarer, who, after many voyages, in deep gratitude has anchored his ship in her 'port for keeps'; this is more than temporary shelter from rough winds and angry seas, it is permanent rest, safety and contentment. Nature, represented by a 'spreading mango tree', seemingly rewards the lovers for their commitment and for the simplicity and sincerity of their love: it drops fruit to be collected in 'the dewy early morning', when love and the world are new and uncontaminated. The serene security of love, however, does not prevent the speaker from having a wayward thought about the unpredictability of life, the recognition of which urges him to confess realistically, 'Not the greatest love story / But humble life with you, / Humble love.' This candid, honest confession in all its simplicity and humility nicely characterizes a love that is full, satisfying and reassuring. Somewhat like art in a modernist world, love here is a rampart against the invasive threat of mutability.

The nature poems showcase Selvon's love for and lasting interiorization of the landscape of his native land: like Tiger in *A Brighter Sun*, he successfully strove 'to impress the landscape on his mind' (125); and in 'Poem in London', the narrator (clearly, one with Selvon), as he roams the streets of London, a cityscape so different from the hills and valleys of the Northern Range, cannot suppress the indelible island experience of 'scarlet immortelle and riotous poui' (*FM* 129) as it tellingly obtrudes on his consciousness. In the earliest nature poem, 'Poui Tree' Selvon singles out the ubiquitous yellow poui – for many the most gorgeous of the island's ornamentals – employing it as a poetic vehicle to remind the reader that the 'essential view' of any experience necessarily involves its life aspect ('yellow blossoms') and its 'lifelessness' ('flowers / Dying on the grass'). To the average Trinidadian, the poui tree is an ordinary vegetational object; to the poet, however, its natural behaviour of presenting contrasting aspects endows it with symbolic significance; it becomes for the poet a symbol of the inevitable mutability of life: one season, it displays it blossomy glory, the next, it is deathly naked, bereft of every leaf and flower (few tropical ornamentals boast of this behaviour). The tree itself exhorts us to follow its example, insisting on the necessity of looking at both sides of the esthetic equation to achieve an integrity of vision inherent in its natural transformation.

In 'Landscape' the poet celebrates what the rainy season does to the island's flora. The beauty of the flowering trees is unmatched 'in any other land' as the 'bare hills [and] cracking earth' of the dry season (January to June) are dramatically transformed into 'such a coloured glory, / Of budding beauty' that only an hyperbole can convey his meaning: an endless vista of yellow blossoms, 'Nothing but flowers / On every limb 'twixt earth and sky.' This is essentially word-painting, of which Selvon is very fond; poet and painter inseparably commingle. Selvon's larger objective is to illustrate the relationship between sky and earth in the tropics, where, as the narrator of *The Jumbie Bird* quietly states, 'In no place but the tropics are life and death so close' (163). Because the colours of life are brighter and more intense in the tropics, death is more keenly felt. Conversely, in 'Rain', the speaker reveals his distaste for the 'wet beauty / Sparkling on trees'. At odds with the season and out of tune with the natural cycle, he misses and longs for the 'sun's friendly warmth' rejecting the 'melancholy draught' that rain offers as it creates a murky, gloomy world. The reader is left wondering why the speaker is so averse to rain because no reason is given and is puzzled by the apparent volte-face in the speaker's response to the rainy season, especially since he has told us in 'Landscape' that it so colourfully and memorably resuscitates the moribund landscape. So intense is his dislike for rain that the external precipitation is a metaphor for '[r]ain falling in [his] heart'; the heartfelt rain creates for the dispirited speaker 'a melancholy world' in which to think is to be '[h]uddled hopelessly' in painful withdrawal. This poem and a few others are, as it were, in excess of the facts; not enough is provided for a reasonable understanding, leaving too much to conjecture.

'Sun' originally published in 1949, was obviously meant to be a counterpart to 'Rain' published some two years before. It is a much more challenging poem that presents the sun as a punitive slave master, whose cruelty and implacability keep the Caribbean people downtrodden, angry and frustrated. Slavery, punishment and death are there because of the sun; but the sun also attracts tourists, with their cultural ignorance and their money, who can never know how desperately close to 'the nothingness of things' slavery has brought the Caribbean. Yet toiling under the merciless tropical sun has engendered in the slaves and their descendants 'red dreams of freedom' the need for revolution to change their wretched plight without any materialization of an abiding yearning to be free, to be human. Somewhat like a confidence man, the sun joins forces with rain to compel the immortelle to bloom in June, giving the landscape a temporary, deceptive beauty, which for a season brightens without and within; like rain, the sun has little to make it attractive to the speaker, who cannot come to terms with the sinister, puzzling world it has created for Caribbean man. 'Discovering tropic', into which 'Sun' was incorporated some twenty-two years later (by John Figueroa for his anthology), is Selvon's longest and most ambitious poem, written with the tourist in mind. Suggesting a specific itinerary and tour of discovery, it invites the visitor to abjure the normal touristy experience and meaningfully immerse oneself in the culture. It urges the tourist to become one with 'coolie' and 'nigger', to enjoy 'mauby' (a refreshing drink made from the bark of the columbrina tree) and 'rock' (a simple, crusty cake) for lunch, and to 'inhale the stench of stink

9

drains'. More and more, adventurous tourists have taken Selvon's advice to heart, as they strive to achieve as authentic a cultural experience as is possible. After the advice and animadversion, the speaker glibly concludes by stating the obvious, 'No one discovers tropic / But many make tropical discoveries.' The final section moves away from 'tall bamboos crisscrossing in the sky' and 'trees in the jungle ... still standing when the sap is dry' to the vexed question of slavery. This, the speaker asseverates, is exclusively an indigenous experience quite inaccessible to the most sincere and progressive tourist, who at best simply moves along the surfaces of things, unable to grasp the native reality of a soul-destroying slavery. Native and tourist, ultimately, live in discrete worlds.

Forming a new category are six poems that reveal Selvon's interest in the world of art and in the creative process. In 'Words and Hearts' the speaker likens the heart to a 'human poet', a poet whose sentiments and experience do not reside 'in the clouds' but are grounded in reality. As the poem makes clear, reality and poetry commingle in life: a walk on dewy grass produces an echoic sound, 'squelching' which becomes grist for the poetic mill; clouds have no sound but their cotton-candy appearance gives the poet the defining phrase, 'dream-clouds'; the richness of the day brings to mind 'a so-blue sky'; water and light in a combined play create 'sparkle-life' on trees; and expectation and desire coalesce to offer the poet 'fairy thoughts' and 'love darling' as he waits for his love. But, according to the speaker, the heart is not involved in the creation of certain words and melodies; such a 'bar' as 'when the pouis bloom again' enjoys an independent life, quite distinct from the promptings of the heart. Not only is the last stanza a recantation of the first and second, but also it appears a contradiction; 'down deep in my heart' cannot be purely intellectual, for human experience does not separate the mind from the heart, however much words tell us so. Ultimately, poetry is the living evidence of this. 'At Tacarigua' is a better-realized poem, dramatizing the divide that separates the speaker from his 'darling' wife. He is able to decode the cryptic language of nature expressed by 'bamboos [that] criss-crossed the sky' and by the 'wind passing / Like a shadow of a ripple'. He assumes or knows that she cannot, though the assumption or knowledge is neither explained nor established.

Selvon had presented a similar domestic dilemma much more memorably in the short story, 'Echo in the Hills' published a few months before: the artist/husband and the uninitiated wife live in different and separate worlds; reasonably, she wants to be treated as just a wife; he, however, sees her as a muse-figure, from whom he draws his inspiration, transforming her into an ethereal being. An adult son, brainwashed by his angry mother, is tutored by his father's explanatory letter, written many years before, into negotiating a posthumous *détente* between his parents. Selvon tones down the situation in the poem and, recognizing the importance of preserving the conjugal relationship, appeals for superhuman help: 'I cry silently to the night / A prayer for you to understand.' In the short story the spouses drift irretrievably apart; in the poem there is the realistic hope that they can 'go together / Down the chasm, up the hill' ideally sharing the impression that nature evokes in two minds moving in unison.

'Lucky Lucre' defines a philistine society that has marginalized the artist / poet, as men and women, worshipping at mammon's altar, have become deaf and blind to the simple joys of life. They prefer to hear 'the jingle-jangle of glittered bits of gold' than to rejoice in 'children's dimpled laughter'; they cannot grasp the richness of 'a simple staying kiss' nor the beauty of 'frangipanis at [their] feet'. The speaker, an advocate for artists, bemoans and resents the fact that 'men who never dreamed a dream / Or symphonized a flower with thought' have pockets that are filled with 'filthy lucre', the central obstacle to the true enjoyment of nature, man and art. Sensing the highly improbable chance poets have of changing a crassly materialistic society, the persona turns his resentment into sarcasm, ending with the image of a miser voluptuously counting his hoard and posing the rhetorical question, 'Who is wiser than a miser?' Conversely, 'The Dive' offers an intriguing illustration of what happens when we habitually live the esthetic experience and perceive the world through the artist's eyes; an ordinary act is transformed into a highly symbolic moment. The speaker is transfixed by a diving woman, who with the 'grace' of a swan on water and the effortless 'gliding' of a raptor approaching its 'valley prey', makes a perfect dive, breaking the surface with 'just the whisper of a ripple'. The fact that she has dived to save a drowning child only increases the rarity and significance of the combination of artful grace and pragmatic purpose; this is the closest Selvon's comes to defining art in his poetry.

'Modern Art' is Selvon's personal response to the phenomenon of modern art and to the chorus of voices that were overwhelmed, puzzled and exasperated by what appeared to be madness without method. Because of its radical departure from the conventions of traditional art, modern art, with its bizarre juxtapositions and irreconcilable paradoxes, struck many as merely a self-indulgent 'chaos' and 'jumble' of images, produced to irritate, shock and alienate the majority of art lovers. Selvon, who spent many an hour discussing art with M. P. Alladin the famous painter and director of the art curriculum for the nation's schools, was well informed about the strengths and excesses of modern art. His ventriloquist speaker is an advocate of modern art in this poem, defending the artist's right to mirror the modern world in unusual collages. He concludes by saying that modern art, like so many other endeavours, will not be appreciated in its time; not because society is philistine and venal, but that it is not yet ready to see and accept its own reflection in phantasmagoric and surreal images.

Quite different from the love poems, the nature poems and the art poems are those that are best understood as existentialist. These reveal the fear, uncertainty and anxiety the fledging writer experiences not about writing but about life itself. These poems were written during the heyday of existentialism, the predominant European philosophy of the late 1940s, to which Selvon, like so many of his generation, was drawn, finding in its naturalistic tenets an attractive option to the smug optimism of rational humanism. It is worth mentioning that Selvon endows Foster, the emerging hero of *An Island is a World* (1955), his first middle-class novel, with an existentialist outlook that engenders intellectual effort but makes significant achievement virtually impossible. For this bourgeois hero, as for the speaker of 'Variation', the 'world unspins / Like the spring of a clock gone mad with winding'. A world spinning out of his control is an insistent trope for Foster whose narrative begins with the image of a world spinning in his brain and ends with a world spinning ahead of him. In this, Selvon's only sonnet, the speaker describes the plight of a man hopelessly lost, like a 'daylight bat / Charting a crazy course in an empty world'; both bat and man can either create fresh courses or can succumb to the emptiness. But the world is spinning for them in the wrong direction ('unpsins') and 'annihilation' is a certainty. Unlike in 'Fear', here there is daylight but the bat / man's eyes cannot decipher reality or truth in the 'blinding light' of the sun.

The existentialist poems begin with 'Success', Selvon's fourth poem, which addresses the double-edged nature of success; this subjective view is a radical departure from conventional thinking about the need to succeed. There is a sense of achievement, but here it is vastly overshadowed by the unnecessary toil of trying to move from one success to another and the 'start of the old restlessness anew'. The endless round of starting and ending, the succession of successes serves only to create a Sisyphean character, who is condemned to constantly repeat the words that delineate his incorrigible condition: 'Always no end, no beginning.' In 'The Dream', too, there is an absurdist world, in which the speaker gains insight into 'the secret' of the 'square circle' but can do nothing with the revelation; as the oneiric vision fades, the speaker experiences the 'tremendous nothingness' of it all. While there are sunshine and daylight in other existentialist poems, 'Fear' is at once the darkest, gloomiest and most frightening of the poems. The speaker fears the ever-present lurking 'unguarded moment' and is unable to assess the value of knowing 'too much or too little'; moreover, he is terrorized by the possibility that 'faith might be insufficient / Yet life might be full'. Instinctively and desperately, he constructs 'little vague gods' only to find that, whether of 'the deep / Of night / Or of the shallow day', they 'all come tumbling / Down'. The insistence on such phrases as 'sinner', 'pagan', 'faith' and 'gods' strongly suggests that the theme of this poem is the insufficiency of religious faith, beliefs and practices. Unlike 'Consolation' where there is the solace of second chances and the probable discovery of 'wiser realms' there is neither hope here, nor faith, nor love;

13

the world is a godless, eternal night, with no light to show the way.

The existentialist poems portray modern man as a lost soul, unable to find meaning and value in success, afraid of the dark, out of tune with nature and light, incapable of finding his place in a world that is beyond his control, and whose only sure end is being reduced to nothing. The controlling thinking of these poems can hardly be the sentiments of a comic writer; as crucial as such thoughts are to an overall assessment of Selvon, the writer, they are not the ones we readily associate with the author of *A Brighter Sun*, *The Lonely Londoners* and *The Housing Lark*, in which, in spite of massive mistakes, loneliness and bewilderment, there are huge opportunities for setting things right and for lasting achievement. These poems reveal the serious, tragic side of Selvon at the beginning of his career, carried away by the initial tide of existentialism. As he matured and the lure of the European philosophy weakened in him, he resumed his belief in traditional optimistic thinking. Though he confesses that he wanted first to be a philosopher, then to be a composer of significant music, 'no stupid calypso or popsong' and lastly, 'to write poetry' ('Preface' to *Foreday Morning*), he must have realized that remaining in the tragic mode as a West Indian writer is self-defeating, given the history of the region; consequently, he gave full rein in his prose fiction to his comic bent.

Selvon's poems are significant for several reasons. First, they reflect the thoughts and concerns of a major fledging writer, who initially was drawn to the composition of music and poetry but eventually moved to prose fiction; from these early pieces we can judge how successful Selvon might have been as a poet. His experimentation with form, his mastery of poetic idiom, and his choice of significant themes strongly indicate, had he wholly committed himself to poetry, that his would have been a potent West Indian poetic voice. Though there is an obvious adherence to the existentialism of Sartre and Camus, there is also a celebration of love, of a transcendent inner serenity ('Wings of Thought'), of marriage, of the native landscape in all its beauty, real and symbolic and even of religious faith ('Consolation'). And like the existentialists, Selvon no doubt saw art as the saving grace in a modernist world of fear, uncertainty and chaos. Except for Foster's perspective in *An Island is a World*, there is nothing in the other novels, short fiction and radio dramas to indicate Selvon's attraction to existentialism. The existentialist poems offer a nihilistic and absurdist experience at odds with the ameliorative pragmatism of Tiger, Romesh, Teena and Andrews. Additionally, because poetry quite often tends to be more confidential than prose fiction, the personal strain in these poems reveals more of the private side of Selvon, especially in the love poems, where there is a confessional mode absent from the novels and present in one or two short pieces.

Moreover, these poems form a lasting and moving record of Selvon's meaningful participation in the fecund flowering of local poetry in the 1940s. Along with Barnabas Ramon-Fortuné, E. M. Roach, Joseph Penco, George Spence, Cecil Grey and Errol Hill (who wrote under the pseudonym of Gaston Lorre), and others, Selvon began to fashion an indigenous poetics, redolent in many ways of the poetry of British mainstream writers, but consciously defined by concerns of national and regional importance. Politics, education, the enhancement of native culture, the need to appreciate the island's flora and fauna, the significance of celebrating the matchless beauty of the tropical landscape, and the cultural importance of appreciating local art and artists were recurring subjects and themes for this coterie of pioneer poets. Their aspirant efforts helped lay the foundation for the more mature and masterful poetic explorations of two succeeding generations.

2

The Radio Dramas

Of the dozens of radio dramas Selvon wrote, only eleven have been published; these are available in two volumes: *El Dorado West One* (a seven-part drama of immigrant life) and *Highway in the Sun* (three plays on the cane trilogy and a fourth adapted from *An Island is a World*).[1] How successful these radio dramas originally were is hard to gauge, since no reports exist; neither has Selvon left any comments. Nevertheless, it is reasonable to assume that listeners, particularly West Indians, who had the time and inclination would have anxiously tuned in; they would have derived a peculiar pleasure in the incongruity of hearing their dialect spoken and culture highlighted on BBC Radio, widely considered in the Caribbean as the home of British culture, embodied in a voice and accent eminently worthy of emulation. Selvon no doubt capitalized on and exploited his fellow West Indian's need to connect intimately and regularly with their warm, colourful culture in a cold, white land. These radio dramas would have done for the listening immigrants what the regular Sunday sessions in the basement apartment did for Moses and 'the boys' in *The Lonely Londoners*, giving them a feeling of being at home away from home, an ambivalent sense of belonging, and making their metropolitan experience much less alienating and dispiriting. The drama experience would have also conceivably given them the satisfaction of knowing that the British were beginning to take West Indian culture seriously, finding in it facets worthy of public broadcast. Additionally, it would have given listeners the curious pleasure of recognizing that what was natural to them was being shared by members of a culture, quite at odds with theirs.

Any critical discussion of the radio dramas must address two concerns: the relationship between them and the novels from which they derive and their worth as radio dramas in themselves.[2] Because they are adapted from the novels, it is virtually impossible not to compare them with the novels, even if only to look at how Selvon transforms his narratives; moreover, because the novels are easily the most familiar of Selvon's works, there will also be an irresistible tendency to hark back to them. Generally speaking, the dramas are less esthetically satisfying than the novels, no doubt because the mediums, criteria, and strategies of the two genres are quite different. Because everything depends on the ear in radio drama, it cannot comfortably accommodate the newsreel technique that provides key background information and a wartime authenticity in *A Brighter Sun*; nor can there be in *Highway in the Sun*, a place for the large symbolic role of the Caroni River in *The Plains of Caroni* that earns for the novel a unique place in Selvon's corpus. Similarly, the weighty matter emerging in the conversations between Hope, Andrews, and Foster, the core of *An Island is a World*, would almost definitely have strained the ear listening to *India Sweet Home*; and Tiger's mental and emotional wrestling, the focus of *Turn Again Tiger*, would have been very difficult to illustrate cogently in the radio drama.

In spite of the fact that Joe's defining moment of violence with Ma Lambie is docked, that Rita is given greater authority, that Sookdeo commits violent suicide as he runs into the path of a bulldozer moving to destroy his garden, and that Tiger's senseless violence on Urmilla after the American guests have left is not retributive, *A Brighter Sun* is nevertheless recognizable in *Highway in the Sun*. But there are other significant differences: there is an overall sense of the anecdotal, as the radio drama lacks the connectedness of the novel; there is no sense that Tiger has matured over a five-year period, nor that he has painfully overcome such tremendous obstacles as a general lack of knowledge, illiteracy and sexual diffidence. There is, too, little sense of the passage of time: *Highway in the Sun* gives the strong impression that the dramatic events occur within a few months. The radio drama spends most of its time in Tall Boy's shop; Tiger's humiliation in the city store, his

17

pleasurable tramcar ride along Maraval Road, and his life-changing hilltop experience in the Botanical Gardens are all omitted. Additionally, the building of the highway does not receive the emphasis promised by the title.

There is, however, greater interaction among the major players in the drama: Rita and Sookdeo do not interact in the novel; here they are allowed to dominate the first scene, trading insults. Whereas the relationship between Tiger and Urmilla is downplayed somewhat, that between her and Rita is given greater focus. They share more of a mother/daughter bond than in the novel, and Rita in the drama is a far more generous neighbour, magnanimous to a fault. Similarly the relationship between Sookdeo and Tiger is essentially that of father and son; widowed, and abandoned by his children, Sookdeo gives everything to Tiger, his words, his time, his advice, and his money. Curiously, Sookdeo an 'indentured labourer' who 'had come from India' to 'work on the white man's plantations' (*ABS* 65) boasts of being 'born and bred in Trinidad' (*HSRD* 8). Such a crucial difference, of course, changes the ethnic equation, blurring the lines of historical continuity between the old Indian and the young Indo-Trinidadian. Additionally, Tall Boy, the village shopkeeper, though harshly referred to as a 'Chinese foreigner' by Sookdeo, is much more acculturated, presented, not as someone differ-ent, but simply as one of the boys, always ready to 'fire one' (have a drink) with Tiger and Sookdeo.

More so than *Highway in the Sun*, *Harvest in Wilderness* is a fairly faithful adaptation of its original novel, retaining the identical characters; however, Souza, the bartender, whose role is negligible, is surprisingly introduced. Although Balgobin's ordeal with the harvester makes him 'go down in history as the saviour of the working masses' (*HW* 169), there is in the radio drama less attention paid to him than to the relationship between Seeta, Petra, and Romesh. Seeta is as domineering as she is in *The Plains of Caroni*, and her unnatural feelings towards Romesh are similarly emphasized. Both Romesh and Petra recognize the inappropriateness of Seeta's hold over her eldest son, though she is not given that level of self-knowledge to recognize that what she is doing is simply wrong. The drama emphasizes much more than the novel the intensity of her political ambitions for Romesh; indeed, she is endowed with insights deeper than anyone else into the nature of an Indo-Trinidadian community far less interested in political power than in financial security. She is the only one who recognizes the importance of political connections, confessing, without recognizing any irony, that 'little things like that put a lot of stupid people in power in Trinidad' (*HW* 152). Her absolute dedication to her son, as in the novel, sets her apart from everyone else in the drama: it is the source of tension between her, and everybody else. Sadly, it does not make her an attractive character: she has marginalized her family, ostracized Balgobin, and is contemptuous of the cane experience all because of her devotion to Romesh. Romesh becomes for her, but for his political indifference, the model Indo-Trinidadian male, a reluctant god of sorts, to whom she is willing to sacrifice all that she is and has.

In both novel and drama, Balgobin's battle with the harvester is the central symbolic incident for the individual, the family members, the community, and the sugar workers of the island. He is the ageing peasant who with his cutlass represents 'the "old" world of cane before mechanization' and he is recognized by all as the greatest cane-cutter alive. Yet the drama does not emphasize, as does the novel, Balgobin's status as a hero who dies in a desperate attempt to give the cane-workers continued life; nor does it underscore the literary epic tradition in which *The Plains of Caroni* so obviously participates. The comparison between the harvester and the Trojan Horse is omitted, as is the ancestry of the epic weapon 'Poya' with its exquisitely sharpened blade, its balata handle, bound by the finest copper wire. Furthermore, the implications of Balgobin's life and death, that he earns an indelible niche in the oral history of the Indo-Trinidadian peasantry, are downplayed in the radio drama. Somewhat similarly, Romesh, though he has the same credentials as in the novel, does not possess a corresponding stature in the drama: he is less sure of himself, weaker, and less decisive in dealing with his emasculating bond with his pretty, officious mother.

Moreover, the title 'The Harvest in Wilderness' remains problematic: it is difficult to understand the choice of 'harvest'. We understand the harvest of experimental cane at the end of

Turn Again Tiger, but we are left wondering where and what the 'harvest' is in Wilderness. To be sure, the cane is about to be harvested; that is the reason why Harrilal enlists Balgobin's assistance. Balgobin dies before the harvest is begun and his death has sparked off strikes on sugar estates across the island. The harvest, therefore, remains to be done. With Balgobin dead, Seeta in mourning, Romesh on the point of emigrating, and the future of manual labour on cane estates in doubt, it is hard to discover any possibility of 'harvest'. For obvious reasons, 'harvester' would have been more appropriate, since the machine is a huge presence, powerful and minatory, the antagonist not only of Balgobin but also of the old way of the life of the cane-cutter.

The drama versions of *Turn Again Tiger* and *An Island is a World*, however, are remarkably different from the novels. In the drama version of *Turn Again Tiger*, Selvon opts to highlight the relationship between Otto and Berta, changing significantly the issues emphasized in the novel. Without a doubt, this central relationship is the source of much humour, making the drama a comic piece in a way that the novel is not. In the novel, the harvest is crucial to the understanding of what Selvon is attempting to achieve: a sense of the true worth of a total community effort. In the drama, the harvest is completed, but this and its implications pale beside the humour of the comedy of errors between Berta and Otto. So central is this relationship that everyone of importance becomes involved in one way or another: Tiger, Urmilla, Singh, and Soylo, who makes it all possible as he procures the feisty, young wife for the older, virgin Chinese shopkeeper.

As Otto's wooing of Berta assumes greater importance in the drama, Tiger's struggle with himself and his book-learning are downplayed. Without reference to the novel, one cannot infer that the testing of Tiger's sufficiency, moral, intellectual and emotional is Selvon's main objective; one deduces that the evolution of Otto as a sexual being and his assertion as a husband comprise the primary intention of the drama. More-over, in the drama there is only one encounter between Doreen and Tiger; the first sighting of the naked woman in the novel is here given to Singh, who alerts an incredulous Tiger to the fact that Doreen bathes naked in the river, and that he has seen 'everything'. The climactic sexual encounter between Tiger and Doreen, which causes the protagonist tremendous emotional and intellectual turmoil in the novel, is transformed into a harmless non-sexual scene in which Tiger kills a venomous coral snake climbing the rock on which a naked Doreen is nonchalantly sunbathing. The relationship between Tiger and Doreen in the drama is made much more deliberate as the young white woman 'takes a perverse delight in tormenting' Tiger to whom she is sexually attracted. A sexual encounter between them, therefore, would have been much less surprising and complicated than in the novel. Perhaps, even a wordless, loveless consummation would have been too risqué for a radio audience in 1970. Additionally, Tiger does not burn his books as he dramatically does in the novel; he gives them to Soylo, who returns them on the family's departure from Five Rivers. Tiger is also unnecessarily insolent to his father whom he often publicly ridicules; his education evidently has not taught him that it is polite to respect elders, especially parents. Sadly, education has given him an arrogance that permits him to humiliate his illiterate father, who is able to deal with his son's insolence only through a physical challenge, which he loses.

Though servile to the white man, Babolal does quite well: his respect for his workers and the eventual success of the experiment elevate him in our esteem. And if Tiger falls in our estimation because of his contemptuous treatment of his father, he restores our confidence in him with his handling of the confrontation with Doreen, with his pragmatic advice to Otto regarding sexual protocol between husband and wife, with his newfound respect for a more assured Urmilla, and with his selflessness in 'teaching the children a-b-c' (*TATRD* 61). If Tiger takes a step backwards in his treatment of Babolal, he takes many steps forward in recognizing that Urmilla has matured and is no longer afraid to speak her mind. Over six years of marriage (oddly, in the 'Characters' we are informed that Tiger is 'married now for a year or so', yet he gives his age to Doreen as twenty-two years old (*TATRD* 76)), Urmilla and Tiger have matured into a creolized couple, who are now content with each other's company and enjoy western music and dancing. They evidently do not know or care for the music of their ethnic group (Indian film songs), so popular then and now with the island's Hindu community.

With Selvon's deliberate veering away from the serious issues that dominate Tiger's struggle in the novel, and his emphasis on the comic and humorous, it is surprising that More Lazy, the self-styled raconteur, in some ways the most intriguing character in *Turn Again Tiger*, is omitted. Including this maverick character would have offered Selvon the opportunity to explore the tremendous comic possibilities of More Lazy's self-imposed philosophy of inaction. The griot's oneiric narrative about the sexual prowess of the black male with the white woman would no doubt have resonated well with an immigrant audience (as it does with the work-bound peasants in the novel), especially if it were related with a typically West Indian relish for the use of particular words. And in omitting Otto's fight with Singh, who enjoys Berta's favours, Selvon robs the Chinese shopkeeper of the opportunity of saving his honour and of earning a special place in the oral history of Five Rivers. Additionally, the ending of the radio drama is anticlimactic: there is no suggestion whatever of what the harvest, real and symbolic, means to the villagers, who work together for the first time to create a unique moment in the evolution of their peasant community. Such omissions make the radio drama a work of diminished esthetic appeal, though we ought to recognize that reading a novel is an experience quite different from listening to a radio drama.

India Sweet Home is the most extreme of all the radio adaptations; although Johnny and Mary are present, *An Island is a World* is not recognizable. The first indication of Selvon's intention is in the significant change he makes to the title; the recommended patriotism and total cultural immersion emphasized in the title of the novel are transformed into the irresistible need to return to 'sweet' India. What makes this novel Selvon's favourite and, in many ways, his most important work, is completely lost, reducing it to a somewhat vapid exercise in self-deception by Johnny. Oddly and disappointingly, Hope, Andrews and Foster, the most fascinating and substantial characters of the novel, are utterly excluded; without their pivotal intellectual interaction, which gives the prose work its verve, seriousness and meaning, the radio drama is quite superficial. In transforming his most serious novel into his most farcical radio drama, Selvon once again shows his predilection for the comic and the humorous. The intellectual demands he makes of Tiger, Moses of *The Lonely Londoners*, and of Romesh, he obviously does not ask of his West Indian audience; they and Selvon, in these radio dramas, are content with a smile, chuckle and guffaw.

In his second volume, Selvon moves away from the island-based dramas of the peasant and middle-class Trinidadian to a seven-part radio drama largely based on *The Lonely Londoners*, with passing reference to *Moses Ascending*. Selvon lays the foundation stone of *El Dorado West One* by having a young black reporter ask Moses, 'Can you tell me something about your early days in Britain in the fifties?' (13). Moses willingly obliges and gives an oral version of the majority of anecdotes and 'ballads' that comprise Selvon's first immigrant novel. The major characters, Galahad, Harris, Cap, Big City, Tolroy, Bart and Tanty are all present; Bob, Moses's batman in *Moses Ascending*, however, reappears in the radio drama with different credentials. Indeed, it is hard to reconcile both Bobs: in the radio drama, he is a colleague at work in the factory and he is Moses's one true friend, who at every turn has his best interests at heart. Bob's illiteracy, his sexual exploits with Brenda and his altercations with Moses over sexual indiscretions are never referred to in the radio drama. He is the one to whom Moses turns for advice and comfort, as West Indian friends constantly thwart the veteran's plans of booking a return passage to Trinidad. The faith and trust Moses loses in his fellow West Indians he readily places in the white Englishman. Similarly, Tanty is the one West Indian who is altogether admirable: she works hard to keep Tolroy's house and home together; she changes the way business is done at the greengrocer's by establishing credit, making things more like they are at home; and though heartlessly conned by Galahad, fulfils her promise of repaying the money she borrows from Moses. To prove her truthfulness and honesty, she goes out of her way to earn the money, and plays a key role in organizing a farewell party for Moses, handing him 'a cheque for fifty pounds' (*EDWO* 154), a sum that is four times as much as the loan.

If, as Crook argues, the beginning of radio drama is absolutely crucial to securing the listener's interest, then Selvon has not been as successful as he might have been.[3] Because the audience of radio drama is not a captive one as is the case with theatre drama, and because the ear assumes ascendancy over the eye, it is vital that the beginning be a high dramatic moment that immediately captures the interest of the listener, who can so easily move on to something else or turn off the radio. Unfortunately, Selvon's beginnings are not likely to pique the interest of the audience; they are weak and unarresting. For instance, he chooses to start *Highway in the Sun* with a verbal exchange between Sookdeo and Rita in Tall Boy's shop. The initial scene is dramatically dull, going nowhere as Rita and Sookdeo abuse each other; Tiger's casual and undramatic entrance does little to stop them. Selvon would have done better by omitting the first two scenes and opening his drama at the third scene with the sound of the bicycle bell and the fateful entrance of the postman bringing the notice that will forever change life in Barataria. The news that the proposed highway is going to mean the loss of many gardens is the beginning Selvon needs: it readily arouses the listener's curiosity about the nature and implications of the change. In radio drama where the listening is everything, the ringing of the bell is an ear-catching device. Additionally, it provides a nice balance to the closing sounds of 'Rum and Coca Cola' coming from the juke-box, a physical reminder of the American presence; like the highway the hit song is a splendid partnership between American know-how (The Andrews Sisters) and Trinidadian creative ingenuity (the composer, Lord Invader).

Similarly, in *El Dorado West One*, the opening scene featuring Moses, the veteran immigrant with an unrivalled wealth of experience and stories, and the neophyte reporter, without name and character, is hardly the dramatic beginning listeners expect; there is no meaningful interaction between these two players. Selvon describes the reporter as a 'young Black Briton' who shares the 'present' with Moses; the listener who anticipates some give-and-take between them is disappointed, since there is no contrast between the new generation of blacks and 'the first generation of arrivants' typified by Moses. The reporter proves expendable as the opening exchange serves no purpose. Selvon could easily have begun with Moses saying, 'Lord ... these boys here once again and I just come off Saturday night-shift in that factory ...' (*EDWO* 13); or, even better, with a shivering Harris inside Moses's room commenting, 'It's terribly foggy out ... You boys sit down here in this cold basement room?' (*EDWO* 14).

If Selvon's understanding of the demands of radio drama is not evident from his beginnings, it is recognizable in the changes he made from one medium to the other. For instance, the violent suicide of Sookdeo desperately running into the path of a moving bulldozer is far more dramatic than his quiet death in the novel and works well in the drama, as human and mechanical sounds merge to illustrate the clash between progress and instinct. However, the need to reveal the dying man's thoughts through voices is an unnecessary repetition which compromises dramatic efficacy. In *El Dorado West One*, Selvon, transforms Galahad into a 'calypsonian trickster figure', selfish, unprincipled, and ready to take advantage of anyone. The empathetic admiration and instinctive connection between Moses and Galahad in *The Lonely Londoners*, evident in two of the veteran's confessions, 'I take a fancy for you, my blood take you' (*LL* 37), and 'Ah, in you I see myself, how I was when I was new to London' (*LL* 85), become in the radio drama a wariness and outright condemnation of Galahad's unscrupulousness. The transformed Galahad, however, is a stronger dramatic character than the less conniving man of the novel. This gives Galahad a truly substantial presence, affording him more time centre-stage, and allowing him greater dramatic mobility than anyone else. Though the Moses of the radio drama suffers no moral diminution as he does in *Moses Ascending* and *Moses Migrating*, and is Selvon's protagonist, it is the picaresque Galahad who steals the spotlight, wheeling and dealing, inveigling and conning everyone, in a desperate bid for survival.

Both *The Lonely Londoners* and *El Dorado West One* contain many humorous episodes; the comedy is much the same in both versions, though it is heightened in the drama as the silent, dormant pages are given voice, accent and tone. What lifts the novel beyond mere comedy and recollection, however, is precisely what is lost in the radio dramas: the pathos of Moses's musing about the grim difficulties of winter and the sensual joys of summer and the poignancy of Moses looking at the reflection of lights in the Thames and thinking he could write a bestseller about his London years. The 'pathos and misery' (*LL* 142) that transfix him in a unique, privileged moment at the very end of the novel are reduced to mere humour and personal reminiscence. The sense that Moses is the archetypal immigrant suffering with his fellow West Indians and bearing their burdens is not emphasized. Nowhere in the radio drama do we find the empathy that Moses confesses to feeling in *The Lonely Londoners*: 'Sometimes, listening to them, he look in each face, and he feel a great compassion for every one of them, as if he live each of their lives, one by one, and the strain and stress come to rest on his shoulders' (*LL* 139).

Selvon admits that he never knew much about the formal art of writing fiction; it is likely that he worked instinctively as well with radio drama, though he confesses to liking the genre 'because there is no limit to where one can place characters' (Nasta, 'Introduction' to *El Dorado West One*). Though Selvon's openings are weak, his sense of character interaction (*Harvest in Wilderness*), of character change (Galahad), and of narrative transformation (*Turn Again Tiger*) is evidence of a solid understanding of the management of dramatic flow, coherence and continuity. Ideally, these plays need to be treated as radio dramas, since they possess their own integrity, autonomy and aesthetic appeal. Whether they are assessed with or without reference to the originals, they ought to be of greater interest to readers, students and critics. Hopefully, the remaining radio dramas will be published soon; this will offer a complete picture of a neglected dimension of Selvon's *oeuvre*; too, it will present new challenges for scholarship that seeks to fill lamentable gaps.

3

Short Fiction

Over a period of 41 years (1946–87), Selvon wrote 61 short fictional pieces. His first completed piece is a short story, 'The Christmas Gift', set in Port of Spain and his last finished work 'Zeppi's Machine' is set in Tacarigua, the north-eastern village where in 1968–9 Selvon spent his longest visit to Trinidad.[1] The majority of his short fictional pieces can be found in two collections: *Ways of Sunlight* (1957) whose 19 pieces were chosen by Selvon himself and *Foreday Morning* (1988) whose 23 selections were collected by Kenneth Ramchand and endorsed by Selvon in a brief but important 'Preface'.[2] In 1987 Jane Grant wrote an introduction to the Longman Caribbean Writers Series edition of *Ways of Sunlight*. Unfortunately, in its primary focus on the author's use of language, it adds little to our understanding of Selvon as a short-story writer. Ramchand, however, in his introduction to the second collection, in addition to providing meaningful insights into individual stories, offers for the first time a categorization of the fictional pieces. He sees them as falling into 'four main areas': 'the immigrant stories like those in *Ways of Sunlight*; personal stories usually dealing with love and set in either Trinidad or London; stories set in rural Trinidad containing characters of Indian origin; finally, stories set in the city or suburbs and containing characters of African origin (representing the Creole world)' (*FM* xiii). In generalized terms and with some reservation, Ramchand's categories are acceptable: there are many exceptions to his last two categories, and his third category comprises pieces that are only superficially love stories. But about his first category, there can be no argument, as these depict the modalities of the West Indian immigrant experience at the heart of the empire. This chapter is the most detailed critical assessment of Selvon's short fictional pieces to date, refining Ramchand's categorization and offering analyses of representative pieces from each category.

Though Selvon sometimes employs the words 'story' and 'episode' to describe one or two of his short fictional narratives, he is especially fond of the term, 'ballad'. Selvon, no doubt, saw his short fictional pieces as falling into two large categories: 'ballads' and others, for which he does not offer a descriptive term. Many of the non-ballads are in effect short stories though Selvon nowhere uses the term. The ballads are loosely structured, light-hearted in tone and comic in style, seeking to provoke humour and laughter. The vast majority of the immigrant stories in *Ways of Sunlight* are ballads and so are a few of the Trinidad-based urban narratives. This is the genre which best reveals Selvon's debt to the calypso, a peculiarly Trinidadian musical creation. In these ballads setting is not crucial and there is little attempt at character development. Even in such longer ballads as 'Calypsonian', the character of Razor Blade, the protagonist, remains static in spite of the fact that he becomes a swindler and a thief in an effort to change his condition as a down-and-out calypsonian. Any real transformation of the protagonist would surely have compromised Selvon's attempt at creating a humorous context. This by no means indicates that the narrative is insubstantial, for Selvon has in mind concerns other than that of development of character.

The short stories, however, show Selvon's mastery of the form. They are tightly structured narratives in which there is a meaningful correlation between setting, character and theme. Yet, in the best of these, there are occasional structural weaknesses. For example, in 'Cane is Bitter', arguably the most significant and predictive of Selvon's rural pieces, the opening paragraph is otiose, providing information that is given elsewhere in the narrative. But Selvon's presentation and style are such that the average reader, swept along by Selvon's mastery of the art of storytelling and seduced by the author's ideology that literature ought to be enjoyed by all, does not detect what to the critic is an obvious weakness.

Another way of categorizing Selvon's short fiction is to

divide it into two obvious large categories: the immigrant narratives and the non-immigrant pieces. The immigrant pieces are necessarily set in London and its environs; the only immigrant narrative that is not London-based is 'Ralphie at the Races', set in Calgary, to which city Selvon had emigrated in 1978 after 28 years in London. The change of setting, expectedly, makes little difference; Selvon's primary concern is to depict the vicissitudes of immigrant life. Ralphie might as well be at an English racetrack; his fortunes would have been the same. Ralphie, a recent immigrant to Calgary, is trying to acculturate himself to life in the city in the oppressive summer heat; if the reversals of expectations and fortunes are indicators of what life in Calgary has in store for him, then he will be a frustrated, wretched individual.

While there is a sameness about the immigrant pieces, there is a huge diversity of setting, theme and character in the Trinidad-based narratives. In the urban narratives, based in Port of Spain, setting creates significant differences: Mrs Bellflent's mansion ('Obeah Man') in St Ann is as vastly different in social context from the pokey 'behind a set of barracks' on Charlotte Street that Gerald Bowen rents ('Rhapsody in Red') as is the bourgeois family scene at Christmas ('The Christmas Gift') from the stark realities of the Dry River community ('Murder Will Out') where all social evils reside. And the wet grass on the hill in the Botanical Gardens ('What's the Use') where the lovers meet is in marked contrast to the streets of Port of Spain, characterized by theft and betrayal ('Boomerang').

Selvon covers the urban landscape in his city-based narratives. Similarly, in the rural narratives, he moves his setting across the island: from Morne Diablo in the deep south, a village which many Trinidadians have never visited ('Pandee Pays a Visit'), to La Romaine, a few miles south of San Fernando ('The Boy Who Made the Rains Come'), to Cross Crossing, a little north of La Romaine ('Cane Is Bitter'), to Las Lomas in the centre of the island ('A Drink of Water'), to Five Rivers to the north ('Holiday in Five Rivers'), to Tacarigua, a mile or two east of Five Rivers ('Zeppi's Machine'), to Sangre Grande, the largest town in the east ('Johnson and the Cascadura') and to Sans Souci, way up on the north-east coast

('The Village Washer'). As in the urban pieces, setting in the rural narratives is crucial to their meaning.

While this categorization is accurate as is one based on style which suggests three groups, dialect, standard and hybrid, it is not as helpful as Ramchand's.[3] But Ramchand's grouping needs to be refined. Among the urban pieces there are two that have as their protagonists Indo-Trinidadians: 'Obeah Man' (*FM* 91–5) and 'Wartime Activities' (*WS* 72–83). In both pieces, the racial origin of the protagonists is given: the obeah man is a 'coolie' (91) and Doolarie, the nursemaid in 'Wartime Activities' is, according to the anonymous narrator, an 'Indian like me' (77). Additionally, there are too many urban narratives that are non-ethnic in that Selvon does not make an issue of ethnicity nor does he provide expected clues to the racial identity of his characters. The ethnicity of the characters in 'Echo in the Hills', 'Rhapsody in Red', 'The Christmas Gift', 'Harper's Happy Christmas', 'Passing Cloud' and 'What's the Use' is never given. And while Selvon informs us that Mr Blade and others are white, he does not tell us whether Gussy, the one-legged caretaker, is white, black or brown, though he is one of the 'natives' ('Gussy and the Boss' (*WS* 94–101)). However, the ethnicity of the characters of 'Calypsonian' (*FM* 142–54) is made clear: Rahamut and his assistant are Indians and Razor Blade and One Foot are Creole or Afro-Trinidadian. While all this is true, it needs to be said that in these pieces Selvon is writing primarily for a local audience from whom he has certain cultural expectations. Though he does from time to time give the racial identity of his characters, he obviously feels that he does not really have to. He expects his readers to know that in Trinidad geographical setting and nomenclature are significant clues to racial identity. For instance, Chin the owner of the parlour in 'Calypsonian' is never called a Chinese but we assume that he is because of his name. All Trinidadians are aware of the significant role the Chinese have played in the evolution of the society; they will always be associated with groceries, laundries, eating places, rural parlours and shops, and gambling. We make this same relatively safe assumption about the other characters in these ballads and short stories. In 'Harper's Happy Christmas' (*FM* 16–19), Harper, Wally, Pedro and Matilda are Afro-Trinidadians, but we conclude that

Boysie is an Indo-Trinidadian because we know that most if not all Boysies are Indo-Trinidadian (Selvon chooses this name for the tall, handsome, creolized Indian in *A Brighter Sun*). We ought to add, though, that nothing about Boysie suggests that he is in any way different from his three friends. And in 'Murder Will Out', setting and nomenclature combine to help us assume that all the characters, Spike Griffith and 'they', are Afro-Trinidadians. Similarly, we assume that Gussy, who lives in Belmont, is Afro-Trinidadian. Ramchand, therefore, is correct when he states that the urban stories depict the 'Creole world', a world that is distinct from the Indo-Trinidadian world of the two urban stories mentioned above and of the majority of the rural narratives.[4]

Since it is impossible in this type of study to look at the narratives individually (as we can in an anthology or collection), the best that can be done is to choose a representative piece or two from the first, second and fourth categories and offer critical interpretations of them to reveal the variety of discourse strategies Selvon employs. The most popular of the immigrant ballads, 'Brackley and the Bed', is, arguably, also the best; from a male perspective it provokes ambivalent humour; female readers, though, will respond with approbation and laughter as Teena adroitly gains a stranglehold over a weak, befuddled Brackley. 'Calypsonian' is easily the most ambitious and successful of the urban narratives. Selvon no doubt created a narrative worthy of his dedicatee and close friend and fellow-writer, Errol Hill, an acknowledged expert on calypso and carnival. Two quite different rural pieces warrant special attention: 'Cane Is Bitter' highlights a crucial moment in the evolution of the Indo-Trinidadian peasantry, while 'A Drink of Water' is a moving human story about Indo-Trinidadians caught in the relentless grip of the worst drought in the memory of the peasant community. The third category comprises just four narratives; all are worth looking at since two focus on the creative process, and two, on the isolation of the artist. These four undoubtedly would have had special significance for Selvon, the writer.

'Brackley and the Bed' (*WS* 139–43) opens with a tired, desperate Brackley looking for a soft bench to rest his weary body and to cogitate on the vagaries of life. It has been some weeks since Teena has arrived in London and has separated him from his bed. The boys respond in a typically Trinidadian way by nicknaming him 'Rockabye', no doubt seeing him reduced to a nestling, whose once-secure perch, as in the nursery rhyme, is wrested from him. Brackley leaves Tobago because he wants to avoid marrying Teena and because things are 'brown' on the island; the narrative makes it clear that marriage to Teena is his destiny. Selvon's casual allusion to Tobago as the island where 'Crusoe used to hang out with Man Friday' (139) introduces a literary figure and theme that occur elsewhere in his works. Crusoe in Defoe's narrative gives up the comfort of 'the middle state' and surrenders to his spirit of adventure; he rebels against bourgeois values, seeking freedom and individuality, and finding them on a Caribbean island (traditionally assumed to be Tobago). In reverse, Brackley leaves the economic hardship of his island home in quest of a bourgeois life in Crusoe's birth-land. Crusoe saves Friday from being eaten by natives, gives him an identity by naming him and makes him his factotum. Teena, like Crusoe, discovers Brackley, becomes at first his servant and then offers him a new life and identity. While Friday peters out of Crusoe's life and narrative, Teena remains to transform Brackley's metropolitan life and to enhance their moral, social and economic chances in an ambivalent London.

Teena arrives in London full of grit and determination, giving Brackley 'tit for tat right away' (140). The quality of her sarcasm in 'You ruling England now? The Queen abdicate?' (140) engenders humour when we grasp the huge gap between the queen in her regal splendour in Buckingham Palace and Brackley in his wretched little room. The humour increases in her improbable use of 'abdicate', though Lord Carreser's popular calypso (1937) had immortalized the abdication of Edward VIII, giving a typically Trinidadian spin to this unique moment in British history. Teena's activities and manner 'mesmerise' Brackley: in other words, she puts him to sleep though she takes away his bed. She is the hypnotist who puts an arrogant, lazy sweetheart under her benign spell, the practitioner with a remedy for the ills of metropolitan life. Brackley, unknowingly entranced, is properly fed for the first time in London, is daily awakened at 6 a.m., is sent off to work, is manipulated into proposing marriage and is acclimatized to a room tidied and arranged almost beyond recognition. Teena, endowed with qualities superior to those of Brackley, quickly grasps the significance of the bed: it is the symbol of Brackley's accustomed way of life, characterized by a lethargic complacency. And she takes to heart the truth of the adage, 'as you make your bed, so shall you lie'. By taking away his bed, she has wrested from him his control over an existence in London that has borne no fruit. She understands that he is a good but misguided man who needs a wife to lead him to a more fulfilling and respectable way of life. In typical male fashion, he resists; but the more resistant he is, the more determined she becomes. Over the weeks she has carefully but quietly orchestrated the new 'pattern' of life for a shell-shocked Brackley.

Hoping to change or destroy Teena's 'pattern', Brackley, on a frosty night, in desperation wakes her and coldly proposes marriage. What he left Tobago to escape ironically becomes the means to Teena's bed. Teena agrees, eliciting from Brackley a promise to come home right after work and not to look at 'white girls'. As he leaves the registry a married man, he can think only of his bed; so powerful is his 'obsession' with the bed that he cannot appreciate or care about the sexual attractiveness of his wife of a few hours. His relationship and marriage are mechanical and non-sexual. He lusts after his bed, impatient to get into it. He thinks not of sleeping with Teena, but of just sleeping, a pattern of behaviour not uncommon among immigrants from warm climates. Teena, herself, is in no hurry to consummate her marriage as she calmly gives to Aunty, newly arrived from Tobago, Brackley's place in her bed. Totally in charge, she plays her version of the waiting game, knowing that she has what she wants and that she will in time reform a lazy, much-too-complacent man into a working husband who appreciates the true meaning of a warm, comfortable bed. She and Brackley have exchanged roles: she has become Crusoe who sails away from home to find fulfilment and a greater sense of purpose; Brackley, however, becomes Man Friday, saved by Teena from self-destruction, compelled to toe the marriage line deliberately drawn by a benignly calculating wife. In Selvon's transposition

33

of Defoe's novel, Crusoe and Friday are united in lasting relationship of mutual benefit. Brackley will, in Teena's good time, gain a new bed, with no contagion from the old, which he will have to share with a caring, focused and future-oriented wife.

Like 'Brackley and the Bed', 'Calypsonian' (*FM* 142–54) is a ballad whose ostensible objective is humour, but Selvon has many other concerns in mind as he describes the plight of Razor Blade, a calypsonian moving through difficult times in Port of Spain. Much like *The Housing Lark*, this hybridized ballad is essentially an oral performance, presented in a scribal form that wonderfully showcases the suppleness of the Trinidad dialect. Selvon's choice of dialect – more often the language of calypso – as his linguistic medium serves to bring both ballad and calypso closer. Like the calypso itself, 'Calypsonian' offers a commentary on social conditions in Trinidad in the late 1940s and early 1950s; indeed, the ballad is in effect a prose version of the two calypsos composed by Razor Blade and One Foot. It records a time of heavy urban unemployment, 'when work scarce like gold' (142), especially for those without 'money . . . or the education business' (148). In such a time men have become picaros, living by their wits, borrowing, stealing and dreaming of being rich and famous. It shows as well the extemporaneous nature of the composition of the early calypso that takes place in as unlikely a place as the back of a 'tailor shop' with the lyrics provided by Razor Blade and the melody by One Foot. This is a collaborative effort by a calypso pioneer and a current calypsonian; it is the combination of the old and the new. Calypsonians are struggling not only because it is their off-season but also because they live in an age when calypso had not yet acquired its latter-day respectability and popularity. Selvon informs the reader of the preference of Trinidadians, of all classes, for such foreign compositions as 'I've Got You Under My Skin' and 'Sentimental Journey'. And it is worth remembering, especially since it highlights his ambivalence, that at the beginning of his artistic career, Selvon, as he makes clear in the 'Preface' to *Foreday Morning*, 'wanted to compose music – not no stupid calypso or popsong – but Nocturne and Symphony and a "Rhapsody in Red"' (vii). Additionally, Selvon, as he so often is, is predictive, foreseeing and proclaiming a time when calypso, the music of Trinidad, will be respected in England and America, and, by extension, globally: a 'time would come people singing calypso all over the world like stupidness' (146). That time is now as Trinidad Carnival and the Dimanche Gras show are televised across the globe and as steelbands and calypsonians make regular tours to Europe and North America.

Unlike 'Calypsonian' which depicts a time when there is massive unemployment for the uneducated, 'Cane is Bitter' (WS 49–63) records a crucial phase in the evolution of the Hindu peasant's attitude towards education. Though an early short story (1950), it is Selvon's most important rural piece, distinctive for its style and theme. It is tightly structured but shows unnecessary repetition of non-essential information: too many words are wasted on Ramlal's sharpening of his 'poya'. Stylistically, too, there are faults: while Ramlal's and Rookmin's dialogue more often than not rings true, Hari's sense of outrage lacks authenticity. Hari, like his siblings (other than Romesh), has never attended school; it is not likely, therefore, that he would say, 'see how he has changed' or 'he is too much of a bigshot to use a cutlass' (53). Most probably as an unschooled child of the 1940s, he would say, 'look how he change' and 'he feel he too big to use a poya'. But these are minor weaknesses; the strengths are many and palpable.

In the rise and fall of the narrative, Selvon employs a style and structure that mirror and reinforce the lie of 'the undulating fields at Cross Crossings estate'. It is a narrative structured by silence and noise, rises and falls and plateaus and peaks. The first three paragraphs, especially the second and third, describe in detail the general happiness of adults and children during 'crop time'. Paragraphs four, five and six create a lull, devoted to describing the physique and features of Ramlal and Rookmin. The following 28 lines of dialogue between husband and wife speed up the narrative flow, creating what might be called a rise. The first 34 lines of the flashback serve as a narrative low, while the dramatic, heated response by Hari, followed by Romesh's angry outburst and lecture create another rise. The final seventeen lines of the longest paragraph of the narrative represent a low, as Romesh realizes that his family have stopped listening to his harangue and he feels 'like an old man' engaged in mere repetition. The final paragraph of the flashback records the parents' decision to 'marry him off' to Doolsie and is a turning point in the narrative. Romesh's arrival from the city school is initially introspection and the realization that nothing ever changes in the village; this causes him, when he puts away his suitcase, to 'sigh like an aged man'. He changes his clothes, goes to the canefield and throws out a friendly challenge to Hari. Frenetic activity among men, women, and children follows as everyone strove 'to outwork each other'. After a satisfying day of hard work comes a most pleasant night of family life:

> And in Ramlal's hut that night there was laughter and song. Everything was all right, they thought. Romesh was his natural self again, the way he swung the cutlass! His younger sisters and brother had never really had anything against him, and now that Hari seemed pleased, they dropped all embarrassment and made fun. 'See, bhai, I make meetai especially for you', his sister said, offering the sweetmeat. (WS 59)

This is a special moment in the life of the family, but it is the lull before the storm. Totally oblivious of the decision to 'marry him off', Romesh very casually announces that he is going to pay Doolsie a visit. A 'sudden silence' grips the family and Ramlal coughs over his pipe, forcing a bemused Romesh to ask, 'Well, what is the matter?' Ramlal's explanation results in the central altercation between parents and child. Night and sleep mark an end to the family quarrel; morning brings quiet and introspection, then Romesh makes a sudden decision to make sure that Ramlal gets the bonus. Romesh hacks savagely and tirelessly until the last cane is cut. Another altercation between Ramlal and Romesh erupts while they are cutting cane: Ramlal demanding obedience and Romesh asserting that he is not getting married and that he is leaving 'after the crop'. The narrative ends by focusing on Doolsie who is too young, inexperienced and unschooled to have an independent opinion about marriage to Romesh. Her mocking friends make fun of her; she becomes angry and in her mind rebels against custom and tradition. The narrative topography, then, in its highs and lows, inclines and flats, and altercations and silences is a fictional equivalent of the rolling surface contours of the Naparima Plains.

'Cane is Bitter' describes a crucial ethnic moment when adult peasants are beginning to think that there is for their children a life that is better than the cane experience. After a hundred years of toiling in the canefields across the island, change comes instinctively, if sneakily. The first step is taken by the hardworking, uneducated parents. Romesh is Selvon's vehicle for his advocacy for change; this is why Romesh, in spite of all the obstacles put in his way, must maximize this unprecedented opportunity and its ameliorative promise. Capitalizing on what is initially seen as good, Romesh becomes a model student in school and in the village. He recognizes the value of what he reads and is taught; he also recognizes what his learning can and must do. It must start with self-transformation, then embrace the transformation of every child in the village, then widen to include every Indo-Trinidadian child in the barrack-yards of the island. Rejecting an early arranged marriage, acquiescence in which means essentially an end to his vision and a betrayal of the golden promise of his education, Romesh finds himself in a huge moral quandary. His allegiance is divided between, on the one hand, family and tradition and, on the other, education and reform. It is the hardest of choices. Romesh is the embodiment of the Indo-Trinidadian recognition of the urgent need to redefine a motherland tradition that is now inappropriate in a new political and social diasporic context. If maintained without compromise, this tradition is inimical to the Indo-Trinidadian's chances for social mobility and acceptance in a plural society, for religious freedom and equality in a polycredal experience, and for intellectual ascendancy in a progressive, competitive world.

It is a time when a few bold adults take the huge step of sending their sons to schools in the city, unaware of the implications of what they are doing. Their vague hope is that their sons will become educated and still retain a strong commitment to Hindu customs. Not educated themselves, the adults cannot know that colonial education and Hindu tradition must clash, creating for parents and sons a dilemma, transacted with considerable agony. Selvon's subject is the gradual interrogation of Hindu custom and tradition. It is not that Romesh is against marriage but that he is against the

Hindu custom of much-too-early arranged marriages, in which the married couple, in their early teens, have no say.

That Romesh is attending school in the city is his mother's idea, for to her education is good thing, even if she assesses its value in purely economic terms: Romesh can become 'a lawyer or doctor', live in a big house with his siblings and parents and have servants. Rookmin is bold enough to challenge tradition, but her boldness blenches before her husband's fear that Romesh is learning 'all those funny things they teach you in school' and that he may 'take a creole wife' (51). The thought of ethnic impurity and the flouting of Hindu custom are too much for her; she capitulates to her husband's myopia and upbraids her defiant son: 'Is the way of our people, is we custom from long time. And you is Indian? The city fool your brains, but you will get back accustom after you married and have children' (60). Romesh, in whom the erotic impulse still lies dormant, and whose appetite for scholastic learning has been insatiably whetted, feels a huge sense of disappointment and betrayal. His parents have sent him to school in the city; they initially encouraged him, now they threaten to remove the one pursuit in his young life that makes real sense.

Selvon creates a young protagonist who has a wisdom, determination and foresight beyond his few years. Unlike Pooran in Ismith Khan's tragic short story, in which the college master destroys the meaning of education, Romesh enjoys his time at the city school and steadfastly refuses to go back to the ways of his parents. Selvon invests much in Romesh, making him his vehicle for criticism of a tradition that is largely irrelevant and counterproductive and for the defiant embodiment of necessary change. In this regard, Romesh resembles Tiger in *A Brighter Sun*, Sarojini in *Those Who Eat the Cascadura* and his namesake in *The Plains of Caroni*. Indeed, it is easy to see the Romesh of *The Plains of Caroni* as the logical culmination of the much younger Romesh of 'Cane is Bitter'. It must be said though that the later Romesh has lost the selfless, philanthropic vision of the younger who insists that the children of his village, and by extension all children, must be educated, must learn about art, politics and science. To this teenage Romesh, education is the solution to the plight of the Hindu peasant, the sure way out of their humdrum and tradition-bound existence that repeats itself from generation to generation. Such is his commitment to educating himself so that he in turn can educate others that he is willing to sacrifice family ties and become a loner. For Romesh cane is not only 'bitter' but also retardative, holding back the meaningful evolution of the Hindu peasants and blinding them to wonderful future opportunities. Both parents, Rookmin and Ramlal, are in Selvon's view, fighting a losing battle as the need for change is experienced, even if in a vague, inarticulate way, by both Rookmin and Doolsie, who though she has not been to school feels an inclination to revolt. Romesh is Selvon's catalyst for interrogation, rebellion and change: the future of the Hindu peasantry rests on his tender shoulders and in the realization of his mature, selfless vision.

'Cane is Bitter' is arguably Selvon's most important and sophisticated Indo-Trinidadian narrative; 'A Drink of Water' (*WS* 102–11) is his most beautifully realized rural narrative. Although it focuses on the plight of several Indo-Trinidadian families caught in the grip of the worst drought in their memory, it is primarily a human story rather than an ethnic one. If the families were of any other race, the meaning of the story would be the same. It is a comic version of an earlier tragic narrative of unrelieved doom, 'The Great Drought' (1948) (*FM* 87–90), in which Sunny's death from typhoid leaves his parents 'desolate' and childless, without solace or purpose. 'A Drink of Water' establishes the rewards of selflessness, the virtue above all that characterizes Manko, the husband/father protagonist. It also illustrates Selvon's philosophy of man outlined throughout the novels: man is given the credentials to succeed if he maximizes the opportunities life offers. In spite of sickness and a 'fatal mistake', Manko, Rannie and Sunny are alive, well and united at the end. The drought takes its toll on vegetation, 'the field was a desolation of drought', on animals and on human beings: '[c]attle were dropping dead in the heat' and 'two children were dead and many more on the sick list' (102–03). As the drought intensifies and farmers become more desperate, there is respite and hope in the water in Rampersad's well. Prayers to 'Parjanya, the rain god', evidently have been answered. The villagers are grateful to god and man, as each one is allowed to drink his fill and take away buckets of water. All are united in the 'miracle they had been praying for' (104).

But this comfortable situation is too good to last. Mrs Rampersad, 'a selfish and crafty woman', is unhappy because her husband's generosity has made others happy. She convinces him to 'put barb wire all around the well', 'set a watchdog to keep guard' and to charge 'a dollar for a bucket and two shillings for half a bucket'. Her selfishness manipulates and transforms him into a greedy man, who takes extreme measures to ensure that he 'make plenty money and come rich' (104); like the 'yellow furnace' sun and typhoid he is prepared to kill if necessary. He and his wife become the human equivalent of the drought and its attendant disease. In a true reading of human nature, Selvon shows the Rampersads securing the hard-earned cash of their fellow-villagers; they create a drought of money for others as they isolate themselves from fellow-workers and destroy the sense of community. One man's luck is everybody's misfortune; one man's greed threatens the lives of all. Manko's potable water is finished, and his cash is all spent on Rampersad's water. When Rannie makes the 'fatal mistake' of drinking unboiled water, Manko is faced with a huge moral dilemma; to offer his wife a chance to live he has to steal Rampersad's well-guarded water. Sunny, unknown to Manko, experiences his own moral dilemma, and decides for himself that not attempting to save his mother's life is worse than contravening his father's warning, 'You must never thief from another man, Sunny. That is a big, big, sin' (106). Both father and son are lucky to escape the bloody attack of the watchdog and the bullet from Rampersad's gun; with buckets empty from jumping over the fence, their brave act seems in vain. But Selvon manipulates his narrative to ensure that their selflessness and courage are rewarded: the sky bursts, rain falls, and Rannie's fever is gone. Such is the comic thrust of the narrative that Selvon resorts to the second use of 'miracle' to describe Manko's understanding of what has happened. The reunion of Manko, Rannie and Sunny leaves no room for chastisement of the Rampersads. Selvon and the community leave them to the pangs of their conscience. With the family together, the parents' hope for Sunny is kept alive. Education can in time nullify the effects of the worst drought:

'He and his wife . . . had been working hard and saving money . . . to send Sunny . . . to college in the city . . . to have plenty of learning . . . [and] be a lawyer or doctor' (103).

The final category of stories is the smallest, comprising only four pieces, three of which were published within the first five years of Selvon's career, the last in 1957. These early narratives are, as Ramchand suggests, love stories. But these are not just love stories: these are quite different from such love stories as 'Johnson and the Cascadura', 'The Christmas Gift', 'Wartime Activities' and 'For the Love of Mabel'. What makes these four pieces unique among the short narratives is their ability to transcend the love interest to present a combined commentary on the creative process as Selvon experienced and understood it. These pieces are by no means monolithic, though it is clear that 'Rhapsody in Red' is closer in form and content to 'Echo in the Hills' and 'My Girl and the City' is similarly closer to 'Poem in London'. The first pair are set in Trinidad, and the second pair are London-based. 'Echo in the Hills' and 'Rhapsody in Red' are, respectively, Selvon's second and third narratives, with the third following hard on the heels of the second. It is therefore tempting to see 'Rhapsody in Red' in some ways as the culmination of 'Echo in the Hills'. Both are essentially depictions of the relationship between artist (specifically, writer and musician) and muse, rendered fictionally as the relationship between husband and wife (the autobiographical implications are clear). But 'Echo in the Hills' (*FM* 62–4) may very well be Selvon's oblique revisioning of the Garden of Eden story; for it is set almost exclusively 'in the garden' (repeated four times), involves a husband and wife and a son who gains crucial knowledge of a lost father while sitting 'under a mango tree on the grass' (63). Nancy, the wife and mother, feels betrayed and deceived by her husband's commitment to his writing; art, then, may be seen as the serpent that surreptitiously enters their world, creates a divide between them and destroys their love and marriage. Nancy greatly influences her son, who, knowing that his father was a writer but not comprehending his world or craft, is guilty of idealism, thinking that the writer is no different from other men:

So I hate my father, because if a man lives with a woman he should make her happy, and when he dies should have given her so much that she is able to laugh while the world weeps, and continue to gather beauty without him.   (*FM* 62–3)

He inherits this youthful idealism from his mother, who wanted no more than an ordinary husband and an ordinary marriage. The sturm and drang of the artist's life turns her off and away from art, beauty, and love. Being treated as a muse rather than as a wife creates in her a fierce resentment, with which she poisons her young son's mind. Though she continually reads her husband's books, all dedicated to her, she cannot 'see light in the darkness . . . [he] left behind' (62). There are none so blind as those who will not see.

In spite of Nancy's self-absorbed blindness, 'Echo in the Hills' establishes the transforming and therapeutic power of the written word. The father's letter, written fourteen years before, has its desired effect: it changes his son's thinking by offering simple but crucial insights into the world of art. Unable to communicate with his wife, he confesses to his son that he was wrong to see Nancy as muse rather than wife, for muse and wife need to be treated differently: 'Maybe my mistake was in thinking of her as a source of inspiration and so I never gave her the things she wanted from life' (64). Both husband and wife become two solitudes: he, moving in a world of imaginative possibilities, she, in the quite reasonable expectation of happiness. But if art can separate writer from family, it can also reconcile and reunite. The son, now 21 years old, is both enlightened and burdened by privileged insights into the artist's world; he must use this epistolary talisman first to descend into the dark world of the dead and then to ascend to the world of a living, bitter mother. There is every reason to believe that he will in time be able to disperse some of the darkness that surrounds Nancy and let in the light of understanding.

Some six weeks after Selvon published 'Echo in the Hills', he wrote a sequel, 'Rhapsody in Red' (*FM* 66–76), a far more substantial and tragic piece. The nondescript garden of 'Echo in the Hills' is replaced by a specific urban setting that takes the reader from the American base at Chaguaramas, to a restaurant on Queen Street, to a room on Charlotte Street, 'behind a set of barracks', to a house in Cascade, to the insane asylum in St Ann. The temporal setting is also more specific: it is a wartime and postwar narrative. What Selvon hinted at in 'Echo in the Hills' is presented more fully in 'Rhapsody in Red'; we follow in sufficient detail the career of Gerald Bowen, the musician protagonist, his aspiration of being a composer, his troubled marriage, the composition of his magnum opus, the growing indifference and resentment of his wife, Muriel, the wilful destruction of his music sheets, his divorce, the attendant madness and his death. Selvon, too, presents a more sophisticated structure: Charles, an old friend of Gerald Bowen and a connoisseur of 'good' music, tells in his uniquely dramatic fashion the tragic story of a great composer. Charles establishes himself as a reliable, trustworthy narrator, who has no axes to grind; consequently, we are more at ease with this man who 'can tell a good story' and we are inclined to listen more attentively in the hope of attaining as full an understanding of the tale as is possible.

Gerald, while at Chaguaramas, seeks to find a way out of Trinidad because Trinidadians cannot appreciate serious music. In this regard he resembles the young Selvon, who 'wanted to compose music – not no stupid calypso or popsong – but Nocturne and Symphony and a "Rhapsody in Red"'. Gerald's and Selvon's musical aspiration, then, is similar if not identical; what Selvon was unable to do musically he attributes to his fictional character. Gerald's early music recalls the painting of Browning's Andrea del Sarto: technically perfect but deficient. For Selvon and Browning, it appears, perfect art is the combination of mastery of the craft and the ability to infuse it with the distillation of one's experience; this is the soul that makes art truly great. Gerald marries Muriel and finds in her both wife and muse, discovering in her 'a foundation' for his music. His good music becomes 'complete' and 'perfect' music as in 'Rhapsody in Red', his masterpiece, into which he pours his life and soul. It is a splendid, 'ethereal' composition, but it comes at a huge price: the philistine resentment of his wife, who tears his musical score into tiny bits after he plays it. The damage to score, marriage and artist is irreparable. The music is destroyed, the marriage ruined, the artist broken in spirit.

With his source of inspiration gone, with his muse rebarbative and traitorous, he quickly goes mad and dies a lonely musician who has known a fleeting moment of artistic fulfilment. 'Rhapsody in Red' ends on a much more tragic note than its predecessor, in which an enlightened son attempts to negotiate between a dead husband and hurt, angry, confused wife. Were it not for Charles's predilection for tale-telling, Gerald Bowen's life, death and music, would be totally forgotten, for an embittered muse/wife makes sure that the product of her inspiration does not exist. While the father in 'Echo in the Hills' can boast of having 'much happiness', Gerald honestly can make no such claim. Selvon in these two narratives establishes that there can be no true marriage of artist and non-artist. As an artist Gerald is allowed to realize his potential though he is not permitted to sustain or maintain it; as a husband, he has been an egregious failure. The union of husband and wife must not be confused with the marriage of artist and muse; the carnal desires of one serve to compromise and repudiate the aesthetic reciprocity of the other.

'Poem in London' and 'My Girl and the City' (the latter celebrates the burgeoning relationship between Selvon and Althea, whom he married some six years later) are different from the other two pieces in the last category in that they deal not with the isolation of the artist but with the creative process. While 'Echo in the Hills' and 'Rhapsody in Red', especially the latter, describe the finished product and its meaning, 'Poem in London' and 'My Girl and the City' comment on the conditions that engender and regulate how, why and when the artist creates. Though an early piece (1951), Selvon never used Standard English more memorably and creatively than in 'Poem in London.' Selvon confessed that Eliot was his favourite poet, and there is ample evidence of his debt to the older poet. Any one who knows Eliot, especially 'Little Gidding', cannot but admit the extent to which Selvon borrows in theme and phrasing. One hears distinct echoes of Eliot in such phrases as 'for to tell you of my beginning, I must tell you of my end' (*FM* 128) and 'We will always only be able to speak of incidents which led to an ending and beginning' (*FM* 130) and 'stumbling over surrealistic phrase catching metaphors in the dancing rays of the sun' (*FM* 132). And although there are echoes of Richard Jefferies (1848–87), whose naturalist writing he admired and attempted to recast in a West Indian mould, Selvon, like so many West Indian authors, cannot escape the influence of Wordsworth, the greatest of the Romantic writers and a staple poet of British colonial education. Selvon, in these two pieces, looks more to Wordsworth than to Eliot and Jefferies. Both Wordsworth and Selvon emphasize the gap between lived experience and the poetic expression of it; both establish the sanctity of nature, described by Selvon as 'the holiness which pervade[s] the atmosphere'. And we readily recognize echoes of Wordsworth in 'A solitary cuckoo gave a call out of the dawn', 'the first rosy flush of dawn surprised the horizon', and 'The morse code, coming to his ears in sweet birdsong, held him enraptured and amazed' (FM 131–2). Both Wordsworth and Selvon record the impact that a weather-affected St Paul's makes on the artist. Wordsworth, 'in a very thoughtful and melancholy state' after visiting an ailing Coleridge, describes his early-morning view of St Paul's as nothing short of a religious experience: '. . . the huge and majestic form of St Pauls, solemnized by a thin mist of falling snow. I cannot say how much I was affected at this unthought-of sight, in such a place and what a blessing I felt . . .'[5] Selvon is less expansive, but no less intense: 'The way St Paul's was half-hidden in the rain . . . How sometimes a surge of greatness could sweep over you when you see something' (WS 174). Additionally, both writers sacralize spots on the Thames: from Westminster Bridge, Wordsworth has a visionary view of the mighty city, immortalized in the famous sonnet; and from the bank of the Thames, Moses enjoys a rarefied, privileged moment of recollection and future possibilities. Fortunately, too, both are personal, expressionistic writers, discernible in their fictive structures, and quite often easily distinguishable from the variety of narrators and personas.

For both writers, the stimulus for artistic creativity comes arbitrarily, at night or day, sometimes when least expected. In *The Excursion*, Wordsworth carefully and consciously creates a topographical pattern that illustrates just how whimsically the imagination operates. It can be stimulated while toiling across a wide common, while ascending a steep incline, while descending a mountain, while gazing at a twofold image of a white ram in a pool or while watching the fiery clouds of a spectacular Lake District sunset. Wordsworth's imaginative stimuli most often come from 'the grand objects of Nature'; Selvon, not as addictively ambulatory as Wordsworth, and living in a quite different age, is constantly surprised while moving about the bustling city, travelling on the tube, or eating fish and chips. For both writers, poetry is the aesthetic mix of 'the spontaneous overflow of powerful feelings' and 'emotion recollected in tranquillity'. It is as arbitrary as it is mysterious; in one instance, Selvon associates it with his muse-like girl: 'I wait for my girl on Waterloo Bridge, and when she comes there is a mighty wind blowing ...' Risking contradiction, Selvon, through the anonymous narrator, asserts that real-life experience is a greater kind of poetry than poetry itself; the first-person narrator of 'My Girl and the City', however, concludes that we move about in a world of words, where words give reality its meaning: 'Everything that happens is words'. Sometimes, ideally, a word defines and legitimizes the experience, though it cannot explain it:

> She never expected that I would still be waiting, but she came on the offchance. I never expected that she would come, but I waited on the offchance.
> Now I have a different word for the thing that happened – an offchance, but that does not explain why it happens, and what it is that really happens. (WS 175)

This is a consummation devoutly to be wished: the yearned-for moment for most writers when experience and verbal expression indissolubly commingle.

Ultimately, Selvon, unlike Wordsworth, is inconclusive, though both see poetry as the product of the marriage of the mind of man and the objects of nature. Where Wordsworth readily defines the pivotal role of the imagination in the creative process and acknowledges the transforming power of poetry, Selvon is content to keep his narrator shuttling between revelation and a lack of knowledge. Like his narrator, Selvon appears to despair of discovering the how and the why; consequently, he takes refuge in a subjective nihilism: 'At last I think I know what it is all about. I move around in a world of words ... One must build on the things that happen ... So

now I weave, I say there was an old man on whose face
wrinkles rivered ... But there was no old man, there was
nothing, and there is never ever anything' (WS 176).

Selvon's ballads and short stories cover a wide range of
themes. The immigrant pieces interrogate in a largely humorous manner the modalities of West Indian life at the centre of
the empire. Only two of these immigrant narratives are
serious; both investigate the creative process; the others
illustrate the integral role humour enjoys in the immigrant's
ability to cope with the metropolitan experience. Since the
emphasis is squarely on theme, there is little variation in the
setting; the primary focus is on the risible, how the West Indian
penchant for humour permits him to hide his pain behind the
kiff-kiff laughter, to give free rein to his libido, to deal with a
variety of immigrant foreigners, to become a confidence-man
and to make a fool of himself. The Trinidad-based pieces are
more varied in setting and more wide-ranging in themes. Even
among the urban narratives, there is a variety of setting that
takes the reader to the botanical gardens, to the streets of Port
of Spain, to rumshops and restaurants, and to colonial houses
in Maraval and Cascade. These settings cover the gamut of
socioeconomic contexts. This is equally true of the rural
narratives: Roger Franklin's estate house in Sangre Grande
stands at one end of the social spectrum, the barrackyard
rooms of the peasants at the other and between them lies a
variety of habitations. The variety of settings is matched by the
variety of themes: the plight of peasants in Las Lomas during
the worst drought in memory, the ousting of an obeah woman
in Sans Souci ('The Village Washer' (WS 64–71)), the inde-
structibility of a symbolic mango tree ('The Mango Tree' (WS
84–93)), the activities among ethnic groups in Five Rivers
('Holiday in Five Rivers' (WS 40–8)), the fruition of a child's
unshakable faith in 'The Mouth Organ' (FM 155–9), the
congruence of coincidence and community belief in 'The Boy
Who Made the Rains Come' (FM 178–81), the presentation of
a crucial phase in the evolution of the Hindu peasantry in
'Cane is Bitter' and belief in folklore and a young girl's flouting
of Hindu custom in 'Johnson and the Cascadura' (WS 1–27).[6]

The themes, characters, settings and styles of the ballads and
short stories are reprised in the longer narratives. As a result,

no study of Selvon's short fiction is complete without an analysis of the varied relationships several of these pieces share with the novels. Such pieces as 'Five Rivers' (1952) and 'Holiday in Five Rivers' (1957), in which More Lazy is first introduced, are incorporated into *Turn Again Tiger*. The Jagroop story is completely transformed into a far more meaningful narrative of the hard-working, idiosyncratic hermit, Soylo, and More Lazy assumes a more crucial and symbolic role. Chin, the 'fat Chinaman', of 'Holiday in Five Rivers' evolves into a more energetic and human character, Otto, who fights Singh for the recovery of his woman, the young Berta. Most importantly, Selvon shifts the primary focus of both short pieces from the theft of Jagroop's mangoes by Govind and Popo to the illustration of how Tiger, his peasant hero, copes with major crises, some of them unprecedented. Teena, the heroine of 'Brackley and the Bed' plays a similarly dominant role in *The Housing Lark* as she takes charge of the boys, puts things in proper order, arranges a day of reckoning, and ensures the eventual success of the plan to buy a house. Selvon does away with Brackley and his metonymic bed, though there is something of Brackley in Battersby, who in the opening scene of the narrative is lying in bed, daydreaming, as he tears off the wallpaper. Additionally, 'Talk' (1951) and 'When Greek Meets Greek' (1965) are incorporated in a slightly modified form into *An Island is a World* and *The Housing Lark*; similarly, 'Roy, Roy' (1950) is incorporated into Selvon's first novel, *A Brighter Sun*, while 'The Baby' is its embryo.

Selvon, sensing that Romesh's narrative in 'Cane Is Bitter' (1951) needed to be continued and concluded, no doubt kept the short story in mind as he wrote *The Plains of Caroni*. To be sure, the two protagonists are not the same character, for so much is different, not the least of which is the older Romesh's family life. An attractive, officious and westernized Seeta in a post-independence Trinidad is as far removed from the homely, frail, tradition-bound Rookmin as we can imagine. And Romesh's vibrant relationship with Petra Wharton, a local white, is the realization of Rookmin's and Ramlal's worst fear. Yet it is not difficult to discern in Selvon's characterization of the older Romesh the advancement and culmination of the scholastic aspirations of the younger boy. Romesh of the novel has secured a university degree and a company scholarship, but he has lost the youthful idealism and philanthropic vision of the high-school student. Though education has changed Romesh virtually beyond recognition, as Rookmin and Ramlal feared, he has Selvon's approbation as he becomes a model for every aspiring young Indo-Trinidadian.

Whereas so much is different in setting, structure, characterization, setting and style between 'Cane Is Bitter' and *The Plains of Caroni* – the former, Selvon's most important rural short story, the latter, the only stylized epic of the Indo-Trinidadian peasantry – it is obvious that 'Come Back to Grenada' (1955) (*FM* 166–77) is the nucleus of Selvon's most famous and important immigrant novel, *The Lonely Londoners*. Though the names are all different, the resemblance between George and Moses, Frederick and Cap, Scottie and Harris, Fatman and Big City, and Gogee and Five past Midnight, is unmistakable. Both George and Moses are veteran immigrants working in 'a factory where they making things to clean pot and pan' (166) and eking out a precarious existence at the heart of the empire. George is considered a 'godfather' to shiploads of immigrants, who 'land up in Paddington from the boat train' and Moses likens himself to a 'liaison officer' and 'welfare officer' welcoming and 'scattering the boys around London' (25). In addition, George's 'basement room ... in Bayswater' and Moses's 'room in the Water' have the same function for the boys on Sunday mornings, a place for 'old talk ... about home in the West Indies, in Trinidad and Jamaica and Barbados and Grenada' (167). In the longer narrative, such phrases as 'like if they going to church' and 'like if it is confession' add an ecclesiastical dimension to what goes on in Moses's room. Yet, whatever spiritual comfort and uplift the boys' experience come from a purely secular message of 'coming together for a old talk, to find out the latest gen, what happening, when is the next fete ...' (138). Even George's decision at the end to 'write to his grandmother and this girl and tell them they best hads forget all about him, because he staying in this big country until he dead' (177) is transformed into Moses's more grandiose musing: his 'wondering if he could ever write a book ... that ... everybody would buy' (142). And the Trinidad vernacular of the 1940s and 1950s that gives 'Come Back to Grenada' its verve, savour and authenticity is reprised in *The Lonely Londoners* to showcase Selvon's revolutionary and unshakable faith in its capacity to meet every exigency of his narrative art.

The short fiction comprises a large and extremely significant component of Selvon's artistic output; it not only lays the structural, stylistic and thematic foundation for his novels but also demonstrates Selvon's mastery of the ballad and short story. These two intra-generic categories allow the gradual emergence of both the comic writer and the serious writer of fiction: the former sympathetically illustrates the role and significance of humour to the island-bound and London-based West Indian, the latter examines facets of the creative experience and draws attention to the need to assess candidly the primary attitudes, beliefs, and concerns of the Indo-Trinidadian peasantry. The short fiction possesses both the quantity and quality to warrant much more critical interest than it has received to date; without doubt, there is enough for at least one book-length study. This ought to have at least two positive results: it will offer insights into Selvon's successful negotiation with the genre; it will also be a corrective to the critical myopia and prejudice that have created a lamentable neglect of works that are indispensable to understanding the mind and art of an exceptionally versatile writer.

4

Novels

The largest share of critical attention on Selvon has been devoted to the novels; this is at best ambivalent. It has rightly concentrated on his most well-known and most important works, but it has inexcusably neglected his other genres. *A Brighter Sun*, Selvon's first peasant novel, and *The Lonely Londoners*, the first immigrant novel, have been the two favourite novels of the critics; consequently, they have received the bulk of criticism. *I Hear Thunder* and *The Plains of Caroni* have been the least popular; the former is the only Selvon novel out of print, and the latter the most underrated and misunderstood of the novels. It is worth noting that foreign critics (Dyer, Tiffin, Nasta, Thieme, Ball, Sindoni among many others) have found the Moses novels of greatest interest; the interest of some of these critics in urbanography, without doubt, has widened and deepened the significance of the Moses trilogy and our understanding of Selvon's limning of 'the great city'. However, the number of critiques of the peasant novels and middle-class novels by non-West Indian critics can be counted on one hand; the exemplary odyssey of the Indo-Trinidadian from canefield and barracks to Parliament and Whitehall appears to be of little interest to them. There exists as well a huge imbalance in the critical focus on the novels. A considerable amount has been written on Selvon's use of language; certainly, much too little has been written on the novels as novels. Surely, *what* a writer says is as important as *how* he chooses to say it. Selvon's critics, often deprecating the artist in favour of the commentator, have found a number of areas of interest in the novels: one group interpret the novels through 'the cultural performance of

51

gender' (Forbes, Espinet, among others); another large group emphasize and analyse his use of the linguistic continuum of Trinidad (Rohlehr, Wyke, Warner-Lewis, Sindoni among others); a third small group investigate the influence of carnival and calypso on the themes and structure of the novels (Fabre, Thieme among others); and a fourth group, while sensitive to Selvon's use of language, stress the significance of the author's fictionalization of cultural, historical and political reality (Barratt, Ramchand, Joseph, Looker, Pouchet Paquet, Dyer, Salick among others).

Wyke, the first critic to produce a book-length study on Selvon, analyses the author's use of 'dialectical and fictional strategies'; there are many useful insights into Selvon's use of voice, tone and language, but there is too little on the novels as novels. The reader wanting to discover the complex ways in which Selvon dovetails theme, setting, characterization and narrative technique in any novel remains disappointed. Sindoni, in the most recent study of Selvon, provides much cultural background information and detailed linguistic analyses of particular passages of the Moses trilogy; however, the primary focus on only three novels is the chief shortcoming of what is otherwise a useful book. Its title, 'Creolizing Culture: A Study on Sam Selvon's Works', promises more than it delivers. Looker, though, offers a postcolonial anatomy of the ten novels, treating each individually; generally worthwhile, his criticism remains unsympathetic and insensitive to the cultural and historical context Selvon consciously establishes, a perfect example being his assessment of Tiger at the end of *A Brighter Sun*, 'Tiger has traveled a long way to realize he is in the same spot' (42). This is a puzzling statement, given Selvon's approbation of his hero's development and the enormous strides Tiger makes on his way to becoming a man. Salick's eclectic reading is a corrective to Wyke's primary emphasis on style, to Sindoni's limited coverage and to Looker's cultural insensitivity; it is culturally grounded, crediting Selvon with an unassailable belief in the aspirations and achievements of Indo-Trinidadians and Afro-Trinidadians of all classes. Selvon, he demonstrates, grasps the enormous literary potential of the ordinary man and endorses his heroic struggle at home and abroad against numerous obstacles to achieve a fair measure of self-actualization.

Selvon's ten novels fall into three distinct categories: the peasant novels, the middle-class novels and the immigrant novels. Selvon establishes these categories very early: a peasant novel (*A Brighter Sun*) is followed by a middle-class novel (*An Island is a World*) which is followed by an immigrant novel (*The Lonely Londoners*). This chronology Selvon also adopts with his next three novels (*Turn Again Tiger, I Hear Thunder,* and *The Housing Lark*). In the remaining four novels, Selvon presents two peasant novels (*The Plains of Caroni* and *Those Who Eat the Cascadura*) followed by two immigrant novels that complete the Moses trilogy (*Moses Ascending* and *Moses Migrating*). The interweave of category and chronology, therefore, must be considered in any assessment of the novels. While chronology does not account for the difference between the two middle-class novels, its significance is essential to understanding the continuity among novels of the same category. Not to grasp the importance of chronology is to disregard the well-orchestrated evolutionary connection between Tiger, Balgobin and Romesh and to miss that the first three peasant novels comprise a cane trilogy with Tiger at its centre. And chronology may well be the key to understanding Selvon's diminution of the later Moses; after 28 years, Selvon had grown tired of London and immigrant life there: 'after some 28 years of inculcating sometimes regurgitating English culture . . . , I was beginning to feel displaced and unfulfilled' (SC no. 226). This disenchantment, made manifest in his move to Calgary in 1978, evidently coloured his characterization of Moses in the last two books of the trilogy. The implications of such words as 'inculcating', 'regurgitating', 'displaced' and 'unfulfilled' may very well be keys to unlock Selvon's deliberate derogation of his anti-hero: it seems as if Selvon takes out his personal sense of feeling displaced, unfulfilled, and jaded on Moses. We may safely surmise that if Selvon had continued the narrative of *The Lonely Londoners* shortly afterwards, instead of waiting nineteen years, he would have presented his immigrant hero in a much more positive light in *Moses Ascending* and *Moses Migrating*.

The peasant novels are island-based and use a largely rural setting to depict the lives of the Indo-Trinidadian peasantry who for over a hundred years toiled in the sugar-cane fields and on cocoa estates across the island. Tiger, Balgobin, Babolal,

Romesh and Sarojini are the main characters Selvon chooses to dramatize the evolution of the Hindu peasant as he moves from a complacent, retrograde view of life to a progressive, future-oriented vision of social and intellectual mobility and of active, meaningful participation in politics. The middle-class novels are also island-based, employing a mixed setting (urban and rural) to delineate the lives of ethnically nondescript bourgeois Trinidadians; many of these professionals are thinkers, sharing ideas on the enhancement of the social, intellectual and political life of the country while others are self-indulgent pleasure-seekers. This is the social class to which Selvon belonged socially and intellectually. It is surprising, then, that these are the least successful novels, although Selvon considered *An Island is a World* his most important novel. Though much of *Moses Migrating* is set in Trinidad, it is quite safe to say that the immigrant novels are set in London and its environs and recount the experience of Afro-West Indian immigrants over three decades at the heart of the empire. Whether intentional or not on Selvon's part, the peasant novels and the immigrant novels admit a further division. There are four peasant novels, the first three of which form a trilogy highlighting the cane experience (although *A Brighter Sun* does not focus on cane as does *Turn Again Tiger* and *The Plains of Caroni*, the two strategically placed references to the cane experience at the beginning (*ABS* 6) and at the end of the novel (*ABS* 215) serve to alert the reader to the importance of the cane experience in the narrative). The fourth novel, set on a cacao estate, presents Selvon's most attractive and balanced heroine. Similarly, three of the immigrant novels form a trilogy centered around the life of Moses Aloetta while the second, with a decisive, resourceful Teena (Selvon's only immigrant heroine) firmly in control of the 'boys', addresses the housing problems the immigrants experienced.

THE PEASANT NOVELS

The cane trilogy dramatizes the gradual evolution of the Indo-Trinidadian peasantry and the role it has played in the enhancement of island life. Tiger is Selvon's representative, yet

54

atypical, peasant; formerly a cane-cutter, he is a hard-working gardener, who longs to know about things beyond gardening and cane, who becomes literate, and who submits a short story to the local newspaper. The Tiger saga really commences in an earlier short story, 'Cane Is Bitter' (1950), in which Selvon first presents a cane-cutting peasant teenager, Romesh, who makes good a rare chance to attend school in the city. He understands the importance of the cane experience to his ethnic group, but also grasps that the implications of education are too crucial to the future of his people not to follow where they lead. This is the dilemma at the heart of the Tiger saga. The Tiger saga continues through Babolal and Tiger (*A Brighter Sun* and *Turn Again Tiger*), reaches a dramatic crescendo in Balgobin (*The Plains of Caroni*) and culminates in the life of Romesh, the university graduate (*The Plains of Caroni*). The young boy's vision and ambitions for the education of every peasant child in 'Cane Is Bitter' are realized in the scholastic achievement of his namesake who is about to leave Trinidad on a company scholarship. On one end of the peasant equation, there are Babolal and Balgobin, representing the traditional way of the cane-cutter, and at the other, there is Romesh, young, creolized and progressive who understands the need for the mechanical harvester. Between these two extremes is Tiger, who is part of the cane experience, who loves gardening and the land but who lifts himself out of ignorance and illiteracy through reading and writing.

A Brighter Sun, a quasi-autobiographical *Bildungsroman*, dramatizes five pivotal years in the life of Tiger Babolal, from his marriage at sixteen to his maturation after the birth of one daughter, a stillborn son, the building of the highway and the writing of a short story. Selvon consciously makes these years coincide with the years of the Second World War; war is not only the historical backdrop against which the drama of Tiger's development unfolds but also a metaphor for Tiger's struggle to vanquish such enemies as illiteracy, ignorance, shame, and loneliness. Both Tiger and the island are beneficiaries of the wealth, engineering skills, and deeper social awareness of the Americans. His American bosses are the ones who offer him promotion because they recognize something different in Tiger and they are the ones who encourage him to develop an interest in local politics. Tiger, an unschooled Chaguanas peasant, according to the dictates of his ethnic group, is married to Urmilla, a teenage bride chosen for him by his parents, in a ceremony that is recognizably Hindu though it is not, as Hindu weddings are, a meatless affair. Selvon, an urban, middle-class Presbyterian by birth and upbringing, confesses in interviews to an ignorance of Hindu custom and ritual; though he had Indo-Trinidadian relatives who lived in the country, he never attended a Hindu wedding. Unwittingly, he creolizes the first auspicious moment in Tiger's life; this, however, proves fortuitous. Selvon consciously continues to push his hero away from traditional Hindu ways by moving him from the heartland of Indo-Trinidadian culture to cosmopolitan Barataria, a village eight miles north of Chaguanas and four miles east of Port of Spain, the capital. Tiger, therefore, for a time leaves the cane experience and 'the sweet wonder of childhood' to become a gardener, to befriend his Afro-Trinidadian neighbours, Joe and Rita Martin, and to leave the garden to work with the Americans in building the highway. This is a short period of tremendous growth for Tiger who has to learn what it is to be a husband, and more importantly, a man. He has to overcome a lack of general knowledge, to best sexual ignorance and diffidence, to consummate his marriage, and to declare and demonstrate his dominance in the home. He also has to establish his maturity and his kinship with his fellow gardeners by learning to smoke and drink rum, a pastime of great importance to Selvon, and one inextricably associated with Tiger's ethnic group and social class. To prove himself a man to Urmilla and to his peasant colleagues is Tiger's greatest challenge at this stage in his life.

As far as Tiger is concerned, to be a man is to acquire sufficient general knowledge; he challenges himself by wanting to know as much as he can. Unlike the much older but illiterate Joe Martin, his Afro-Trinidadian neighbour, confidant and friend, Tiger equates immaturity not with a lack of experience but with a want of knowledge, especially of the sort found in books. Selvon creates an epistemological novel of sorts, transferring his own middle-class drive for knowledge onto his peasant hero, endowing him with a fierce and insatiable desire to pull himself out of the quagmire of illiteracy and ignorance.

Burning the midnight oil, literally and figuratively, he plods through Henry's elementary-school primers, teaching himself to read and write, finding a voluptuous satisfaction in coming to terms with the exciting possibilities of language. Seeking a balanced experience, he toils by day in his garden, drinks hard with his fellow gardeners and at night assiduously increases his knowledge of words. Though his fascination with words for their own sake leads him into such silliness as defining cigarettes to a nonplussed Urmilla as 'small cylinders of narcotic rolled in paper', he perseveres with his reading, going so far as to buy 'a book about roads' to understand better the experience of his work with the Americans. Like Selvon, Tiger is instinctively drawn to words, language and narrative; he 'slowly and painfully [begins] to write about how they had garden, but the Americans came and they had to move' (*ABS* 127), thereby unknowingly giving structure and meaning to his life in Barataria. For his interest in words and narrative, Selvon rewards his hero, giving him an admirable drive to succeed and to overcome a stultifying ignorance, accepted by all his fellow-peasants except Sookdeo, his old gardener mentor who teaches him the value of increasing his vocabulary. After his embarrassment in the store in Port of Spain, when the white woman is attended to ahead of him, he is given a compensatory tramcar ride to view the architectural splendour of 'The Magnificent Seven' that adorn Maraval Road and an unprecedented visionary experience on the highest topographical point in the novel. It is a Wordsworthian moment of privilege, as he enjoys the panoramic view of the Gulf of Paria and the north-west peninsula and revels in the parti-colored sunset sky blooded by a flight of scarlet ibises coming home to roost on the trees of the Caroni swamp. At one with cosmic consciousness for the first time, in this epiphany (many similar moments occur in the works of Richard Jefferies to whom Selvon acknowledged a conscious debt) the hero begins to understand the value of knowledge, the need to put his life into proper perspective and the wisdom of planning for the future.

Though Selvon's presentation of his hero is somewhat idealistic, his commitment to realism compels him to chastise Tiger when he does wrong. The greatest reproof comes when Tiger, nurtured in a culture of violence (Tiger is regularly beaten by his parents and Joe comes of age through a violent exchange with Ma Lambie), verbally abuses Urmilla, likening her cosmeticized face, suggested, encouraged and insisted on by Rita, to that of a Port of Spain whore. He denigrates his wife's complaisance as she spares no effort preparing for his American guests. In his befuddled state, he cannot control his anger and need to establish his authority; he kicks her across the face and in her stomach while she writhes in pain on the floor. This is a defining moment for Tiger. Though he never expresses remorse to Urmilla, in the months following his wilful attack, he, Selvon's thinking peasant, begins to mull over his recent behaviour, growing increasingly concerned about Urmilla's deteriorating health. Her constant groaning, coughing and fighting to breathe are too much for him, compelling him to confess and act, 'I going to get a doctor. I can't bear to see you suffering so, man' (*ABS* 180). Along with this, comes the realization that '[e]verything had been going wrong . . . and that it was only himself to blame' and more tellingly that the 'feeling like a disaster was about to take place, and it was all his fault, everything that had happened, he was the cause of it' (*ABS* 193). He experiences 'fear', 'trembling' and 'shame' but for Selvon this is not enough; he must further punish his errant hero. Tiger's physical abuse of his wife causes her to give birth to a stillborn son, denying him what he most wanted. Without the benefit of this shibboleth of his ethnic group, he must find his way to manhood guided by a parenting Selvon. Moreover, he secretly blames Rita for the death of his son and stops talking to her and Joe; with Sookdeo dead, he now has no friends. The highway is completed and formally opened and Tiger is no longer employed. He has lost his son, lost his neighbours and best friends, lost his surrogate father, lost his job; this combined loss drives him to his social and emotional nadir.

Tiger has come a long way in these four years; knowledge and experience have given him an exemplary resilience and will to re-ascend. Showing neither arrogance nor self-aggrandizement, he quietly takes charge, rebuilding not only his house but also his sharded life. Needing to be alone to come to terms with his guilty feelings, he insists that Urmilla and Chandra go for a holiday in Chaguanas. Now a solitary vagrant he wanders all over the village, wrestling with his jostling thoughts and emotions. Though Tiger appears to have put his books away for a time, he has taken the advice of his American guests on the importance of politics to heart. From his confession to them, 'I don't pay much attention to politics and thing', he, carefully manipulated by Selvon, has reached a point where he constantly thinks of politics. Just before the baby is born, he engages Joe in a conversation about the nature of government, and, roundly boasts, 'Boy, one day I go become a politician. Is politics that build a country . . .' (*ABS* 195). And on the way to Port of Spain, riding a donkey cart, he and Juggernauth, an old villager, share a significant moment which reveals Tiger's deepening interest in and commitment to politics. Juggernauth wants him when he becomes a politician 'to fight for Indian rights' and Tiger, displaying the benefit of his reading and thinking, wisely replies, 'Everybody rights, not only Indian'. (To know that in the 1940s, when the novel is set, and in the early 1950s, when the novel is published, Indo-Trinidadians were not part of mainstream politics in Trinidad is to grasp how optimistic and predictive Selvon is of the future of Tiger's ethnic group.) Essentially alone now, he cannot but cogitate and engage in self-censure, 'I should talk to Joe Martin and Rita . . . Is not their fault, is nobody fault but mine. Why I so stupid . . . I too shame' (*ABS* 204). Selvon approves of his protagonist's maturity and sincerity and helps him on his way to recovery. The fractured friendship is soon mended, even if the reconciliation is initiated by Rita; Joe and other villagers begin to assist in the building of the house and a well-rested, happy Urmilla returns to Barataria, though Chandra stays in Chaguanas. Urmilla's return marks a new chapter in her relationship with Tiger: their conversation reveals the beginning of a meaningful sharing of thoughts and feelings, a mutual respect, a real partnership in which she is no longer afraid of physical and verbal abuse (of course, with Tiger's positive evolution, her fears are unfounded) or of speaking her mind.

All of this coincides with the official declaration of peace. Tiger, in a real sense, out of a gnawing compunction and profound appreciation of all that he has experienced and caused, declares his personal armistice. His war with Urmilla, with Joe and Rita and with himself appears to be over. He has come a long way in his five years in Barataria: his house is 'almost completed' and he gives Urmilla money to furnish it; he returns to gardening and to the land; and he achieves at last an appreciable contentment in his marriage – 'He would go home and Urmilla would show him the furniture she bought. They would eat dinner; he would sit and read, or they would talk old things' (*ABS* 214). At 21, with a new sense of marriage as a partnership, with a modern house that would be 'standing years after it was built', with his memory mulling over his Barataria experience, with a firm commitment to politics and with his short story, 'written about the highway', completed and posted, Tiger, well poised to face new challenges, is entitled to feel an immense satisfaction. His final confident affirmation, 'Now is a good time to plant corn' (*ABS* 215), a momentous transformation of his initial helpless question to Ramlal, 'What I must do?' (*ABS* 7), is Selvon's recognition of how far Tiger has travelled on the road to self-actualization. He has become, after the trials and tests, a man who knows about planting, about being a father and husband, about the need for political involvement, about words, language and writing. He has become a brighter sun/son, blazing for Indo-Trinidadian peasants an exemplary trail that leads to education, social mobility, creolization and political participation and lighting up a path of endless possibilities for individual, community and nation.

Six years later, after a middle-class novel and an immigrant novel, Selvon resumes the cane saga in *Turn Again Tiger* as Tiger agrees to be bookkeeper for his father who is given the unprecedented responsibility of managing an acre of experimental cane in Five Rivers, a village some five miles east of Barataria. Tiger's decision to become part of the cane equation again is surprising for at least two reasons: firstly, his attitude towards cane, 'He hated cane. Cane had been the destiny of his father and his father's father. Cane had brought them from the banks of the Ganges to toil in the burning sun. And even when those days were over, most of them stayed shackled to the estates' (*TAT* 1); secondly, because it roundly contradicts his resolve at the end of *A Brighter Sun* as he shares a light moment with Urmilla, 'You think I going back to work in the canefields again? Not if is the last thing in the world to do' (*ABS* 209).

Though the decision to help his father is ultimately a personal one, it is, as are so many island decisions among Tiger's ethnic group, a combination of several factors: Babolal's embodiment of the cane experience, Joe's matter-of-fact response, Urmilla's reasonable deduction that he is 'deciding not to go', the villagers' assumption that he is going and his wish to change the 'pattern' and 'the sameness of life'. Tiger's decision is Selvon's way of telling us that for the Hindu peasant the cane experience, the cultural crucible in which he has been nurtured, cannot be votively whelmed; it is ineradicable. It also gives Selvon the opportunity to continue the narrative about his best-known peasant hero, whose first narrative had indelibly intrigued and impressed readers and infused the much-needed strength and vitality into a sluggish literature, struggling for voice, focus and acceptance.

Tiger's second sally into the canefields is quite different from the first as a sixteen-year old boy in Chaguanas: the venue is Five Rivers, a village 'far in the bush'. He has now greater experience as man, father, husband, gardener and road-builder, gathered over a five-year period and he has gained an impressive measure of literacy that allows him to read Plato, Shakespeare and Omar Khayam (Selvon never discloses the extent to which Tiger understands these celebrated authors; nevertheless his interest in and ability to read them is altogether admirable). Tiger agrees to become part of a cane experiment; yet *Turn Again Tiger* is ostensibly about experimental cane. In a real sense, it is about Selvon's experiment with a narrative different from its prequel for it proves hugely experimental for Tiger who must test the practicability of the knowledge he has gained from his reading. Moreover, it a serious experiment for Babolal who is given his first opportunity to manage a cane plantation; a novel experiment for Otto, who obtains a feisty wife who must be brought into line; an unthinkable experiment for More Lazy who eventually decides to normalize his life by finding work; and a courageous experiment for Urmilla who leads the women and compels Otto to stop giving their husbands rum on credit. For the village, too, it is a definitive experiment in working together to achieve a common purpose. It is therefore a testing time, a struggle, an ordeal for individual, family and community.

Small wonder, then, that 'fight' and 'wrestle' occur frequently and are key concepts in this novel.

Though often at odds with his father, with whom he fights physically and ideologically, Tiger's real antagonist is a restless, intellectual discontent, embodied by Doreen Robinson the young white wife of the overseer. (Selvon, given the plot, must have taken a huge risk with the choice of the name Robinson; Harold Robinson was for many years in Selvon's time a well-known overseer of sugar estates. He later became very influential in the administration of agriculture and in politics in Trinidad.) They are therefore destined to meet, interact and to return to their accustomed, individual lives. He first encounters her accidentally as she sits naked on a rock 'under a slight drop' from which water tumbles. Instinctively, Tiger becomes the voyeur, drawing 'himself into a clump of bamboo not to be seen'; 'breathing deeply' and experiencing a welter of emotions, he views her nakedness, 'her breast proud and pointed, and the hair of her head was golden' (*TAT* 49). Selvon never establishes whether Tiger is sexually aroused; we are encouraged to deduce that the sheer surprise, the instinctive fear of the white woman and the inherited ambivalent attitude towards her commingle at this moment to quell any erotic feelings Tiger might experience. Reasoning that he has done nothing to be 'guilty' of, Tiger walks on 'looking straight ahead'. Doreen sees him and dives into the shallow pool, looking at him and making him feel 'as if he were the naked one in the water'. When she shouts 'Hallo' Tiger scampers away like a guilty thing upon a summons. Just before he espies Doreen, he had discovered the overseer's 'painted, city-looking house' and this had set off a train of thoughts about the power and authority of the white overseer 'making all the money' and 'screwing the young Indian girls in the cane'. Selvon presents him with an opportunity to even the scores; instead, he is afraid, 'full of shame' that he 'made a mistake in fleeing'. Suddenly he begins to slash at anything within reach, no doubt mortified that Doreen's nonchalance had rendered him impotent. All his rationalizations gel into one inescapable deduction: 'it had nothing to do with colour or the generation of servility that was behind him', 'he had fled because she was a woman, a naked woman and because he was a man' (*TAT* 52).

But Tiger is wrong. It is precisely because she is white and the overseer's wife that he flees; he has failed his first experiment. In spite of his hatred of cane, his resentment towards the white overseer and his renegade thinking that he does not fear the white man, he was 'angered most of all by the feeling of being unable to cope' (*TAT* 53).

Tiger is able to overcome the emotional and mental turmoil temporarily, but on payday as Doreen rides to the front of the house with her husband, Tiger loses his equilibrium, 'Her presence upset Tiger completely and disrupted his plan of behavior' (*TAT* 58). Still, Tiger handles himself well: he engages Doreen in conversation and mixes a drink for her, feeling 'good with himself'. This stands him in excellent stead when he is sent to the supervisor's house to work and plant a garden. He is the epitome of self-control even though Doreen wears 'a yellow piece of cloth across her breast' and shorts tight enough to reveal 'the outline of her panties'; he is able to withstand what, in Selvon's mind, is sexual teasing. But try as he may, Tiger cannot quell his desire for Doreen, a desire that 'was burning hotter than ever' and he goes to the house everyday hoping to get a glimpse of her, thus increasing his wanting her.

The second encounter at the river is expectedly different; though not quite a tryst, both sense its impendency and are better prepared for it. As Tiger leaves Doreen's yard, 'he saw her looking at him through the window' and no doubt, driven by desire, she follows him. Tiger, wracked by an emotional turmoil, muses, 'If the chance come, I know what I go do' (*TAT* 145). Although the wordless consummation takes place, Tiger's anger and murderous thoughts seem wholly inappropriate as Doreen is ready, composed and willing to take the initiative. Without saying anything and with a 'finality' in her eyes she coolly walks away as if she had anticipated and rehearsed the encounter; 'She had come silently, and in silence they had done it . . .' In the first encounter, Doreen dives into the pool to hide her embarrassment and cover her nakedness; in the second meeting, it is Tiger who needs to dive; 'he dived and stayed below for as long as he could, motionless, until his ears rung' (*TAT* 148). This has nothing to do with shame, nakedness or triumph. It is an act of cleansing. The first dive does not quite do it, lacking the requisite integrity; it leaves his head 'warm' and his body 'cold'. It takes a second dive and an atavistic abrading with sand and mud and a lying prostrate at the head of the pool, 'where the river meandered over clean rocks and stones' (*TAT* 148). Shutting his eyes tight, he blocks out all except the singing of the river and achieves what he hopes for, a serenity and closure. Doreen fades out of the narrative as neither Tiger nor Selvon has any further need of her. She satisfies a renegade curiosity in Tiger, a dull, vague wanting. Desire for her never harasses him again. This time his experiment is successful; he has struggled with the demon of white untouchability and in his own hazy way, even if only to settle an old grudge, evened the score between him and the sexual rapacity of the white overseer. (Tiger and Selvon, it seems, are at odds here, as the young man is manipulated in doing something, the reason for which he does not fully understand.) Tiger, therefore, is made to represent a new generation of peasants: young, literate, desirous of righting wrongs, eradicating the evils of a colonial past, thereby making possible the huge scholastic and social progress of a younger generation, represented by Romesh (*The Plains of Caroni*).

Except for Tiger, More Lazy is the most intriguing character in *Turn Again Tiger*; he is also the most comic. He is unique, wandering from village to village, never finding the need to wash his face, to change his clothes, or to work. He arrives with no significant past or future in Five Rivers and 'anchor[s] himself under a spreading salmon [*sic*] tree in the centre of the village' (*TAT* 99).[2] Born Theodore Sebastian, but never having any use for the name, he rechristens himself 'More Lazy', a soubriquet which nicely mirrors his philosophy of inaction; indeed with a penchant for using words, he finds in this moniker the linguistic equivalent of his modus vivendi. No doubt, this endears him to both Tiger and Selvon. In a village of hardworking peasants, More Lazy initially becomes an object of curiosity, then of ridicule, then of disgust. Only Tiger takes the time to get to know the 'idler'. When the practical joke of carrying him to the bank of the river as he pretends to be fast asleep is over and the perpetrators realize that he has taken it 'in good spirit', they warm towards him and Tiger offers a conciliatory drink which he readily accepts. Embraced by the indulgent villagers and establishing his right to be under the centric samaan tree, he becomes the griot, telling 'stories which he had picked up on his travels'. Night after night, this chronic idler seduces the industrious villagers with his oneiric narratives that entertain them and introduce them to an experience so distant from their working in the fields. In recompense he receives food and money. Tiger, doing for him what Sookdeo once did for him, introduces him to the world of words. Because Tiger burns his books and turns his back on traditional knowledge and engages in a partnership with More Lazy, it is not unreasonable to deduce that the idler's way of life is an indigenous replacement for Plato and Shakespeare. Significantly, he takes up abode under a samaan tree, a mighty tree, which like the Afro-Trinidadian and the Indo-Trinidadian, has long been naturalized in Trinidad. The acceptance of the villagers and Tiger's generous friendship transform the vagabond raconteur into an active individual who speaks words he has never uttered before, 'Tiger, get a job for me, man. I can't stay in the village alone' (*TAT* 174). With Soylo doing the bookwork, More Lazy and the women bundling cane and Tiger and the men cutting, the harvest of experimental cane is at once a literal and a symbolic one. It is metaphor for the enormous benefit that derives from true cooperation by the entire community; undoubtedly, this is an ideal for both Tiger and Selvon.

Turn Again Tiger is ultimately a successful experiment for author and characters. Selvon moves Tiger forward in time but back into the historical experience of cane, no doubt to illustrate the pragmatic truth of his hero's musing at the outset of the narrative, 'Sometimes a step back better than staying in the same place: the next time you move forward you might be able to make a big stride and go way pass where you was before' (*TAT* 7). Significantly, this occurs in the only flashback in the novel as Tiger, sitting on the hill overlooking the village of Five Rivers, 'his life spread out before him', struggles to make up his mind to leave Barataria and the 'pattern'. Though he is concerned neither with 'pattern' nor knowledge as his son is, Babolal's experiment in Five Rivers results in a 'permanent promotion' moving him up from cutting cane to managing

it. And though Otto's experiment with marriage brings unan-
ticipated problems, he wins the day and the respect of his
flighty wife and the community when he defends his honour
by challenging Singh and breaking his arm. As with Tiger, this
encounter brings closure and equanimity to the village shopkeeper, whose fight with the Indian cane-cutter earns him a
niche in the oral history of the community. The same is true of
Urmilla's leadership of the delegation of wives to Otto's to stop
the shopkeeper from crediting rum to the husbands. Her
experiment, too, of having Berta as her best friend results in
her further creolization as she enjoys dancing (and dreams that
Berta is teaching her to jive and do all the fancy steps), and
gives up sandals in favour of high heels though she keeps her
sari. Pregnant with her third child, and wishing for Chandra's
sake 'that she knew how to read and write' she will in all
probability give Tiger the son he craves, the right to which he
has earned. More Lazy's experiment with language and
manual labour also reaps rich dividends, affording 'the negro'
a new sense of belonging, importance and community in a
village of Indo-Trinidadians; this experience of work and
payment transforms him into someone who is 'giving serious
consideration to the idea a permanent job'. Selvon's experiment is most successful for Tiger, who has done what he
promised: he has assisted with the management of the cane
and been part of a successful harvest. But it has been much
more for Selvon's hero: he has lived in another village and has
been allowed to interact not only with the villagers and More
Lazy but also with the white supervisor and his wife, thereby
deepening his social experience and teaching him to manage
desire. Tiger makes sure progress over a lustrum in *A Brighter
Sun* but he makes greater strides during the year at Five Rivers.
On the threshold of a political career when he returns to
Barataria, since the committee has chosen him as its representative who will liaise with the government on the needs of his
community, he must, in Joe's words, 'turn again' and resume
his interest in books and 'dem things'. This is the first crucial
step in fulfilling a resolution he made to Joe towards the end
of *A Brighter Sun*, 'One day, boy, I go become a politician' (195).
Keeping his interest in narrative alive, he will no doubt find
the need to write another story about his soul-defining

experience in Five Rivers. After all that has happened, Tiger cannot seriously rue his decision to help his father; indeed, he has helped everyone in so many different ways, men, women and children, changing their humdrum lives and emerging in the process a stronger, more confident and wiser man.

Selvon took the opportunity to continue and conclude the story of his best-known peasant hero in *The Plains of Caroni*, the writing of which was paid for by Tate & Lyle, the British sugar conglomerate. In 1969, Selvon spent eight months in Tacarigua (his longest stay in Trinidad since he migrated in 1950) and completed the final novel of the cane trilogy. *The Plains of Caroni* is unique among Selvon's novels in that it is his only work that aspires to be epic: the opening 37 lines, two crucial references to heroic literature, the description of Balgobin's cutlass, the implications and effect of his battle with the harvester, and the oblique allusion to the *urbs condita* theme unmistakably indicate its epic intentions. Selvon mingles river and song in his deftest opening, at least three strains commingle to form a vast composite melody. The river that has witnessed the social history of the island from the days of the indigenous Amerindians, to the coming of Spanish, of the British, of African slaves and lastly of Indian indentured labourers, like the epic poet, 'sings' of what it has experienced and internalized over the centuries. The repository of island history, the Caroni River, chants its tutelary hymn of arrival and departure, of toil and betrayal, of struggle and triumph, of defiance and death. And the oral history as told by the unlettered peasants who live and labour along the banks of the island's longest river is the primary epic. Selvon's interpretation of the integral role the Indo-Trinidadian peasants have played in the progress of the island's economy and their contribution to the cultural mosaic is, in effect, the secondary epic.

Tiger lives, dies and is reborn, as it were, in the two protagonists of *The Plains of Caroni*: Balgobin, the oldest, greatest cane-cutter and Romesh his son, a young university graduate with a bright future in management. Balgobin, who represents the old way of the cane-cutter, is an obsolescent hero, desperately attempting to hold back the hands of the clock and preserve the only way of life he knows. He is the archetypal cane-cutter, having 'planted and reaped more cane than any other man in Trinidad'. He is also the epitome of the cane experience: 'His whole body oozed odour. Not the smell of sweat and dirt – these were overwhelmed by the sweet smell of molasses, and sugar-cane, and rum. By smell alone, he was a part of the sugar plantation' (*POC* 10). Selvon's description of Balgobin's 'artistic hand . . . more suited to paintbrush or pen' suggests that he stands apart from his fraternity and that he has transformed the commonplace activity into an art, of which he is the consummate master. He is brought by his younger brother, Harrilal, to Wilderness to help with the harvest; he is brought by Selvon to do battle with the mechanical harvester. The relationship between the protagonist and antagonist is more clearly defined and presented than in *Turn Again Tiger*, where we are unsure of what actually motivates the consummation. The mechanical harvester threatens the livelihood, continuity and humanity of the traditional cane-cutter, represented by Balgobin. It is a mortal confrontation of the machine and human, of past and future, of faith in technology and belief in man. This is a defining fictional and historical moment for protagonist, community and cane-cutters across the island. This product of man's technological invention comes one morning 'lumbering like a cumbersome juggernaut', accompanied by 'a Land-Rover . . . a special loading truck . . . and a mobile welding unit'. It looks to many villagers 'like some metal Trojan Horse', a magic machine capable of doing the work of eighty-eight men (67–8). The use of 'juggernaut' and 'Trojan Horse' invokes two quite different traditions of heroic literature, the Hindu and the Classical: the former referring to the image of Vishnu carried on a cart, under which devotees would hurl themselves to be crushed; the latter, the most famous symbol of treachery during the Trojan War. (The presence of these two references raises questions about Selvon's control of his narrative perspective; the first reference belongs to the anonymous narrator who evidently knows what a 'juggernaut' is and perhaps where it is first depicted; the second reference is far more problematic since it belongs to the peasants ('looks to many villagers'). It is not realistic to think that Balgobin and his fellow cane-cutters would know of the 'Trojan Horse' or would make the comparison).

To help Balgobin do battle with the mechanical harvester is his 'poya', an epic weapon that has been part and parcel of his experience as a cane-cutter for 'sixty years', with a balata handle, 'bound to the steel with the finest copper wire he could get'. Accustomed to certain patterns of movement and fixed to a fixed routine of action, 'poya' in action 'seemed to have a life of its own', rebelling if a stranger held it and wounding those who scoffed at its power. Like most epic weapons, it has pedigree, ancestry and a history that mingles with the mythological: 'It had descended from a strain of buccaneers; its ancestors had tasted real blood. Poya knew that several of his friends and relatives kept the buccaneering spirit alive, particularly on the banks of the Caroni, and in the Indian villages . . .' (POC 76). The relationship between 'poya' and Balgobin is one of epic reciprocity, heroic symbiosis: it has made him the most famous, adulated, and sought-after cane-cutter on the island and he has, 'wander[ing] all over the island from sugar estate to sugar estate' (POC 10–11), made it the most celebrated, feared and successful cutlass. Inseparable from the hand that has wielded it for six decades, it has been ever dependable, bestowing in epic fashion an invincibility on Balgobin. Its most momentous test is against the harvester which, like the 'juggernaut', will in time crush to death the largely Hindu peasantry and which, like the Trojan Horse, is seen as a perfidious gift from the gods of Industry. Its last and definitive battle is its first and only confrontation with a metal 'giant monster'. As Balgobin brings it down 'with all his strength against the side of the machine', 'Poya ricocheted, springing back with a whine', incurring an honourable but not fatal six-inch-deep 'wound' (POC 77–8). Selvon's virtual humanization of 'poya' suggests its inseparability from Balgobin, in particular, and from the Indo-Trinidadian peasantry, in general; life for the Hindu peasant is unimaginable without his 'poya'. The vast amount of time the cane-cutter devotes to honing, cleaning and maintaining the integrity of his 'poya' is in direct proportion to its tremendous significance among the ethnic group; while there is neither awe nor reverence, there is care and protection that approximates religious devotion for this simple implement.[3]

If the 'poya', though badly wounded, lives to cut more cane,

Balgobin engages in his last ordeal; he utterly destroys his enemy, wins the battle but loses both the war and his life. Though he is an obsolescent hero, he is given a final opportunity for heroism, dying as he has always lived, a solitary man, with a tremendous faith in the worth of the peasantry. If Santiago, in Ernest Hemingway's *The Old Man and the Sea*, with whom he shares many similarities, is overtaken and made redundant by the historical process, after his three-day ordeal with the largest fish ever seen or heard of, Balgobin's battle makes him an epic hero, putting Wilderness on the map and making him the centre of island-wide adulation and concern. If Santiago in time is forgotten by his fishing community and by the younger fisherman with their radios and power boats, Balgobin's prowess as a cane-cutter nonpareil and a fearless fighter for peasant continuity earns him an indelible niche in the oral history of the peasants who live along the banks of the Caroni River. Selvon's irony appears intentional: Balgobin has heroically sacrificed all to the sugar industry whose mascot, the harvester, mechanically brings about his death and eventually the demise of manual labour.

If in *The Plains of Caroni*, Balgobin stands at one end of the cane equation, then Romesh stands at the other. Father and son, their propinquity revealed at the very end, are ideologically pitted against each other, though they, unlike Tiger and Babolal in *Turn Again Tiger*, are never physically at odds. Romesh is the emergent hero of *The Plains of Caroni*, fulfilling fully the scholastic ambitions of Tiger and his namesake in 'Cane Is Bitter' and representing the apotheosis of the peasant. He starts by cutting cane, takes a university degree, joins management, and is on the verge of leaving Trinidad on a company scholarship. In his characterization, Selvon delineates the historical evolution of the Hindu peasant. If he does not quite fulfil the younger Romesh's vision for the children of his ethnic group and for all peasant children, the older Romesh is allowed to enjoy the kind of creolization that Tiger desires and Selvon enjoyed. Tiger, of course, marries at sixteen, is a father a year later and, though he chafes occasionally about the unfair burden of his marriage, neither finds the courage nor the trepidation to leave his wife and child. Selvon is more sympathetic to Romesh, who is in love with Petra Wharton, a local white university student as free of racial prejudice as he is. They are intellectually matched, liberal-minded and sexually compatible though, as we would expect, Petra has social and political connections to which Romesh can only aspire but which he, if Seeta has her way, will capitalize on.

As the emergent hero, young and future-oriented, Romesh faces two antagonists, a *Weltanschauung* epitomized by his father and internalized by the peasantry and the officious machinations of his restless, westernized mother. His epic weapon is education and an indomitable belief in the future. Whereas Balgobin is obsessively complacent about his cane-cutting experience, Romesh understands the implications of the use of the harvester to the enhanced solidity of the sugar industry. Unlike Balgobin, he appears not to be solicitous about the harvester's displacement of the peasant worker. Indeed, nothing, except his name, suggests that Romesh is a Hindu peasant: his university education, his easy creolization, his anxiously frustrating relationship with his mother and his non-committal response to his father's cremation all indicate that he has travelled too far from his roots to ever find them again. The characterization of Balgobin and more so of Romesh is Selvon's literary vehicle for the transmission of his grasp of and vision for a post-Independence nation. *The Plains of Caroni* contains Selvon's strongest criticism of island life – driving habits that endanger lives of pedestrians, driver and passengers, chronic environmental pollution, the dress of civil servants with the battery of coloured pens in their plastic-lined breast pockets, the wearing of a tie, the 'emblem of slavery', the pretension of carrying empty briefcases to impress others, the inclination to mind other people's business, and the facile nomenclature of adding 'Trini' to almost everything. The novel also establishes the tragic futility of being stuck in the past and the practical wisdom of accepting the inevitability of the historical process that insists on change and progress. Balgobin has done all that his experience and thinking allow him to do for his ethnic group; with the old hero gone, the future of peasant and industry may be said to be in the control of Romesh who, after the scholarship and necessary managerial experience, will conceivably be in charge.

In permitting Romesh to rediscover, albeit accidentally,

Petra and to rekindle their sexual relationship, Selvon offers his young hero, beset by saucy doubts and fears about his ambivalent response to his mother's unnatural overtures, a chance to normalize his sexual feelings. Petra, though much younger, is better balanced than the still beautiful 40-year-old Seeta, who has marginalized her husband and two sons, and lives only for Romesh whose academic and political future becomes the lodestar of her life. It is Petra who confronts Romesh with the unnaturalness of the relationship between mother and son and informs him that he has 'an Oedipus'. She insists on the need to assert his individuality and emotional fortitude if he is to extricate himself from mother's unyielding grasp. Petra becomes, in spite of a youthful beauty, a Sybil of sorts providing the wayfaring epic hero with the information he vitally needs if he is to succeed in his quest for mastery of his life. Romesh finds the strength to defy his mother in his resolve to leave Wilderness. The endorsement by Forbes, the white company manager, of his ability as a scientific researcher working on the production of premium-grade yellow sugar crystals, Petra's promise to wait for him to return after the scholarship, and the passing of an era with the death of Balgobin coalesce to establish the brightest of futures for Romesh. With the death of Balgobin and the use of the harvester, Popo, Romesh's youngest brother who wants to emulate Balgobin, will never get a chance to give a heroic display of what the master taught him about the art of cane-cutting. However much we regret this, we acknowledge the invaluable contribution that Balgobin and his generation have made to the success of the sugar-cane industry and to the vitality of the island's economy, and we recognize Selvon's need to have the old cane-cutter establish in his heroic battle against an inhuman antagonist his 'glorious episode of history'. Balgobin's life and death will in time become an essential part of the song sung by the Caroni River and by the peasants who live along its banks. With an irony Selvon could not have anticipated, Romesh's exemplary progress from canefield through university to management ought to be seen as the final chapter of the Indo-Trinidadian cane narrative which ended in 2003 with the permanent closure of Caroni 1975.

Selvon's fourth and final peasant novel, *Those Who Eat the*

Cascadura, is unique in several ways: it is the only one of the author's novels to be set on a cacao plantation; it is the final and most important of three versions of a short story first published in 1948, then revised in 1957; it is the only Selvon novel to highlight a romantic relationship between a white Englishman and a native Hindu girl; it is Selvon's solitary sally into romance; it is the only novel in the corpus to investigate the supersensory world of obeah and island folklore; and it presents his most rounded and admirable heroine who embodies a heroism that is quite different from that of Tiger, Balgobin and Romesh. No doubt, Selvon felt that he had said in his three previous peasant novels all that he needed to say about the cane experience. Perhaps, too, he chose to set his final peasant novel on a cacao estate because this was the agricultural sector, other than sugar cane, in which the Indo-Trinidadian peasantry made a significant contribution. He also uses it as a vehicle for his ongoing criticism of Hindu custom that retards and quite often disregards the education of children, especially girls.

Using a well-known couplet by Allister Macmillan, a white English historian, 'Those who eat the cascadura will, the native legend says, / Wheresoever they may wander, end in Trinidad their days', as his epigraph, Selvon constructs a narrative, somewhat like Ismith Khan's *The Obeah Man* (1964), that focuses on the nature and power of local superstition. The evolution of the novel indicates how deliberately Selvon manipulates the storyline. 'Johnson and the Cascadura' is the shortest and simplest of the three versions of the cascadura narrative. It is essentially a masculine narrative about the relationship among three men: the anonymous narrator and overseer, Franklin, the owner of the cacao estate, and Garry Johnson, Franklin's friend who is on holiday. This monolithic narrative has neither androgyny, nor eroticism, nor a love interest. Moreover, it is marred by unnecessary description that further retards a slow-moving plot, by stylistic awkwardness, by inexcusable shifts in tenses, and by such solecisms as 'he looks around at Franklin and I' and an insignificant structure: Garry Johnson arrives, stays a while on the cocoa estate, leaves for England, returns to Trinidad and dies before the doctor arrives. This seemingly fulfils the promise of the legend embedded in the couplet, memorized by every student in Selvon's day. Selvon investigates the truth and seriousness of what without doubt would have been a humorous couplet when it was initially conceived of by someone who, at best, would have been sceptical, at worst, dismissive of the claims of his literary lines. 'Johnson and the Cascadura' is a juvenile piece, not really important, except as a gauge of the narrative progress Selvon makes over a period of 24 years.

The second version, with the same title, initially appeared in *Ways of Sunlight*, Selvon's first collection of short stories. This version is five times as long and equally more substantial; indeed this reads like a completely different narrative. The geographical setting remains much the same, though the temporal setting is vague, sometime after the global fall in cocoa prices (late 1920s). Such significant issues as the treatment of Hindu children by their parents, the attitude to interracial relationships, ethnicity and love are introduced to contribute to a far more complex and aesthetically satisfying narrative; additionally, the four-part structure works well. The two primary white players remain unchanged, while the overseer is teasingly called Sam and given a far more comprehensive role: he is narrator, friend to Garry, confidant to Franklin and he is in love with Urmilla. She is a young and independent Indian girl of arresting beauty, who has defied her father's wishes by avoiding marriage and neutralized sexual overtures by villagers. She has kept Sam at bay and is introduced as Garry's lover, setting tongues wagging and emotions soaring. Both lovers, driven by a passion they hardly comprehend, totally ignore ethnic practice and expectations, turning the cocoa estate into their erotic playground. That their love-making is not private, witnessed by her father and Sam, among others, in no way stains its innocence or sincerity. It is a mutually fulfilling relationship, disapproved of by Franklin, Sam, Sookdeo and the village but endorsed by Selvon. Believing absolutely in the truth of the native legend of the cascadura, Urmilla prepares 'curried cascadoo' for Garry just before he leaves for England. She virtually takes charge of her destiny, ensuring Garry's return, though he now suffers from a terminal blood condition. Selvon repays her faith in the supersensory world as the lovers are to be married; it is not unreasonable to assume that her visit to the local obeahman for a cure for Garry's illness will be successful. The ending, though ambivalent, is hopeful, turning, with Selvon's approbation, the tragic story of the first version, into a comic narrative. Selvon realized quite early in his career that his strength as a writer lies in his mastery of comic narratives.

The second version of the short story, rather than the first, is the basis of the novel, *Those Who Eat the Cascadura*; the third is the best and most substantial version of the narrative. Selvon makes several significant changes: unlike both short stories, the novel is a third-person narrative; the setting is more expansive, moving out of the cacao estate to Balandra Bay far up the east coast; Eloisa, Franklin's housekeeper, is introduced and given an important role; Prekash, betrothed to Sarojini, is the most educated villager, disliked by everyone, including Selvon and he takes over from Sam as overseer; Franklin's character is deepened and darkened in his relationships with Kayshee and Kamalla, giving him a character dimension at odds with the high esteem in which he is held by the entire village; Kamalla is introduced as a foil of sorts to Sarojini; and Manko, the village obeahman, merely alluded to at the end of the second version incarnates into a major character. The novel introduces a devastating hurricane that forces everyone to take stock of things and it also shows Selvon's interest in obeah, though his attitude to it is ambivalent, while Sarojini's is absolute. This highlights a problem inherent in his characterization of Sarojini, whose attitude, thinking and behaviour he thoroughly endorses.

Selvon's primary intention in this novel is to establish a female heroism embodied in his beautiful female character and his most attractive heroine. What happens on and to the cacao estate appears secondary to this intention; consequently, he creates a heroine who can do no wrong, for what are often weaknesses in a character are strengths for Sarojini as Selvon fashions a Pygmalion relationship between himself and his heroine. (It is worth remembering that the novel is dedicated to Althea, Selvon's second wife, a woman, like Sarojini, of arresting beauty.) Sarojini is an exceptionally beautiful young woman, whose riveting beauty is recognized and acknowledged by all, men and women, Indo-Trinidadian and Afro-Trinidadian and white, adult and child, visitor and native.

Moreover, her external pulchritude is a correlative index of an inner beauty and innocence. Although she knows 'depression' and 'dejection', she is in charge of most of the situations in which she finds herself. When she is helpless, Selvon steps in to assist his heroine and to save her from serious physical injury and cowardly rape. Her defiance of Hindu custom, her belief that she was born for better things than marriage to Prekash, her intuitive management of the relationship with Garry and her absolute faith in the powers of the obeahman all pay rich dividends, as she achieves an admirable level of self-actualization, though she does not marry Garry. Her abiding dream of something big happening to her materializes in the arrival, sojourn and departure of the English visitor and her lover, Garry Johnson.

Sarojini's heroism is quite different from that of Balgobin, Romesh and Tiger. Balgobin defines his heroism in the mastery of the cane cutter's art, in his unrivalled knowledge of the cane experience and in his definitive ordeal with the harvester. Romesh establishes his heroism in his exemplary evolution from cane cutter to university graduate, to be part of management, to scholarship winner, to the possibility of participation in the political process. Tiger, the most convincing of the heroes, burdened by an early marriage, baffled by diffidence, troubled by a lack of knowledge even of simple things, is driven by an atypical drive to overcome the barriers that ignorance and inexperience have placed in his path. In *Turn Again Tiger*, we see just how far Tiger's epistemological efforts have brought him: he is able to read Plato, Omar Khyam and Shakespeare, no mean achievement for an illiterate, unschooled peasant. Yet we are made aware of how little this intellectual advance prepares him for the realities of peasant life in Five Rivers. Still, with steps forwards, mis-steps and steps backward, he is rewarded with a balance and new understanding of what the future holds as he takes his first decisive political step as his community's representative who will liaise with the government on the needs of Barataria. We therefore can see in Romesh's intellectual achievement and Seeta's relentless hope that her son will enter politics and establish a name for himself the fulfilment of Tiger's aspirations in both fields of endeavour.

None of these assets are given to Sarojini: she lacks significant experience beyond the cacao plantation, is unschooled and has no interest in reading, has to borrow clothes, even underwear, has no expertise except in cooking, cleaning and washing, and is not allowed even a passing interest in politics. She is the epitome of the peasant life in all its complacent simplicity, a simplicity, incidentally, that would hardly have existed in a post-independence Trinidad with radio, television and compulsory education. All this, of course, is a function of Selvon's intention to create his only romance, in which man meets woman, they fall instantly in love, they have a carefree romance that does not lead to marriage, yet in which there is little room for regret or recrimination. The relationship between an Indo-Trinidadian female peasant and a white male visitor in a predominantly Hindu village expectedly incurs the censure of the villagers who are bound to custom, ritual and tradition. Though in other social contexts, this relationship between white and Indo-Trinidadian would be considered a way to upward mobility to the native, here it is definitely, even for Kamalla, the least attractive of the female characters, outrageous and unacceptable. But Selvon is squarely on the side of his heroine whom he protects at the cost of the credibility of his fiction.

Selvon resists the temptation to write a comprehensive romance by ending his narrative with ambiguity. After indulging in a love affair that has scandalized Sans Souci, Garry leaves for England without a promise to return. Marriage is out of the question, because there are many things to work out in England. Roger sees the positive side of Garry's return, suggesting that in time he will forget all and if that does not happen he can return in partnership with him. After making love in the moonlight on the very spot they consummated their relationship and after making 'sad love' in bed at the big house, Sarojini leaves the bed, placing the donkey-eye, dutifully hexed by Manko, in Garry's hand. Selvon chooses to end his narrative with a chapter that recalls the opening pages of the novel. Though Sarojini is not certain that 'there was a life beginning in her' we are encouraged to believe that she is with child in Selvon's insistence on natural sexuality and procreation: 'Two leghorns were still missing, but there was a brood of chickens with one of the hens' (*TWEC* 180). Though the final tableau of the novel is open-ended and ambiguous with Sarojini unable to distinguish between her donkey-eye and Dummy's, we sense that all will be well with her, as with the cacao estate after the devastating hurricane. Selvon, throughout the narrative, has endorsed his heroine's beliefs and aspirations, has approved her choices and behaviour and has protected her from physical injury, telling calumny, and rape. Garry's admission to Roger that neither Sarojini nor he can forget what they have shared intimates that Sarojini's dream of finding an appropriate husband and family will materialize, particularly since the complaisant Englishman, half believing in its efficacy, enjoys the cascadura that his lover has specially and hopefully prepared for him.

THE MIDDLE-CLASS NOVELS

Selvon's two middle-class novels, *An Island is a World* and *I Hear Thunder*, depict the lives of the island bourgeoisie in the postwar era. Ethnicity is a significant issue in the peasant novels; in the middle-class novels it is not. Selvon's major characters in *I Hear Thunder* are ethnically nondescript, though we are told that Adrian is Indo-Trinidadian, Mark Afro-Trinidadian and Randolph Bellings is a local white. There is virtually no difference in the behaviour of Adrian and Randolph, although the latter enjoys a social mobility and advantage denied to Adrian. Mark, unlike both Randolph and Adrian, has studied abroad and returns with a medical degree and a white wife; Adrian is a travelling representative for a canning firm, while Randolph has inherited his family's wealth and does not need to work. Similarly in *An Island is a World*, the major characters are racially defined but ethnically nondescript; this does not work well for Selvon. Both Foster and Jennifer are Indo-Trinidadians, while Andrews is Afro-Trinidadian (Father Hope is not described racially); all are creolized and westernized to the point where there is no meaningful difference in their behaviour. Among the lesser characters there are those to whom race and ethnicity are central issues. Selvon's detailed description of Seeta's dress and cooking habits indicate that she is a traditional Indo-Trinidadian woman who is proud of her ancestry; the disappointment, disgrace and anger she and Motilal, her husband, feel when they learn that Polly, their daughter, is pregnant by Randolph are functions of their fierce pride in race and ethnicity. In *An Island is a World*, Johnny, a drunkard and arsonist, who leads the Back to India group, leaves for India, accompanied by a dutiful wife and young grandson who do not share the old man's obsession. Jennifer, his younger daughter, out of a deep commitment to her island home, stays behind and marries Foster. From such a couple, Selvon intimates, will come a generation of Trinidadians who in time will grow to appreciate and embrace the practical wisdom imbedded in the declaration of the words of the title, *An Island is a World*.

An Island is a World is Selvon's most serious novel, and in some ways, his most important work; it is also, as Selvon himself confesses, his favourite. But it is neither his most successful nor interesting novel. It is, as Naipaul notes in his review of the novel, a *roman à thèse*: Andrews, Hope and Foster represent philosophical and ideological positions. Andrews is Selvon's political man, practical, balanced and solution-oriented; Hope is Selvon's theological man, intellectual and selflessly committed to his unlettered parishioners. Foster is Selvon's hero, restlessly struggling to overcome an existentialist outlook to attain a maturity, conviction and commitment that are second nature to Andrews and Hope. From the frequent discussions among these three friends emerges the thought of the novel and from the characters of these three major players we can extrapolate Selvon's ideal middle-class citizen: someone who is politically involved, finding solutions to the nation's problems, who is intellectually active, searching for fresh ideas on which to establish new systems to guide our living, and who is engaged in an on-going struggle to attain self-actualization. As the title suggests, Trinidad ought to be seen as a place that offers opportunities for the constant enhancement of self, community and nation, fostering a meaningful patriotism that maximizes the possibilities for nation-building. Although Hope disappears from the narrative (whether he accidentally falls off the cliff or commits suicide is left up to the reader), he has established in his exemplary life a pattern of commitment and selflessness to be emulated by both Andrews and Foster. He dies to allow Foster to accept the burden of leadership of which he knows he is capable.

Selvon's second middle-class novel, *I Hear Thunder* (1963) is his least successful novel: very simply, it goes nowhere. He confesses in 'Autobiographical Essay': '*I Hear Thunder* gave me more trouble than any of my other works . . . I felt I was out of touch with Trinidad after staying away for so long' (SC no. 88). It lacks the thought and purpose of *An Island is a World*, showing little concern for theme or characterization. In a culture, in which a 'drowsy complacency' characterizes middle-class living, and in which men and women are equally unfaithful to their partners, there is perhaps some point to prove in being celibate. Adrian, lacking sufficient will and commitment after a life of endless affairs and no love, decides to be faithful for a year. Polly, his girlfriend, is suspicious of his abstention from sex, and makes herself available to Randolph, a predatory lothario, the least attractive of all the characters, given neither conscience nor humanity. In the final week of a year in which Adrian had been less than honest with Polly and himself, his best friend, Mark, returns from abroad with a medical degree and an attractive white wife, Joyce. Adrian is immediately attracted to her and contemplates having sex with her, should the opportunity arise. This is in total disregard of his friendship with Mark and of the implications of betrayal. Selvon creates the opportunity while Mark, Joyce, Adrian and Polly are holidaying in Mayaro, a fishing village on the south-eastern coast of the island. Joyce puts up little resistance as she and Adrian have sex on the beach in a cold and calculating act that recalls the loveless consummation between Tiger and Doreen in *Turn Again Tiger*. Tiger's deliberate act, however, occurs within a symbolic political/historical context, carefully created by Selvon; Adrian's is bereft of any symbolism that raises it beyond mere satisfaction of lust. Whereas Tiger is Selvon's thinking peasant, working assiduously to improve himself and his family's chances, Adrian is a complacent, colourless bourgeois who creates no intellectual challenges for himself. In the bourgeois equation, Foster and Andrews stand at one end, Adrian and Randolph, at the other.

Unlike Randolph, Adrian does have a conscience, which bothers him somewhat as he contemplates confessing his infidelity to Mark. Selvon, unfortunately, does little to convince us of Adrian's emotional agony or sincerity. He confesses to a remarkably composed Mark, who nonchalantly counters with his own confession that Polly is pregnant with Randolph's child. Nobody seems unduly disturbed by these betrayals, as days after the two couples enjoy themselves playing Carnival. Mark and Joyce stay together, and there is no discussion between them of her infidelity. Mark appears suspiciously asexual; work and contemplation of a political career, it seems, have replaced his sexual interest in Joyce, who like Polly, is hardly worth any genuine affection. As a carnival-weary Mark leaves for home with Joyce, he invites Adrian to visit the next day to 'talk about things' and Joyce invites Polly to '[c]ome for lunch tomorrow'. The final tableau shows Adrian too tired to move from the pavement, unwilling to disturb a sleeping Polly, who 'was a dead weight in his arms'; the symbolism is all to patent. Though the narrative ends with the thought that 'some befuddled Trinidadian didn't realize it was Ash Wednesday and time for repentance', we sense that Selvon has fashioned a fictional world in which the 'chaos and confusion' of Carnival is too attractive, even soul-destroying, bringing out excessive participation in someone as moderate and even-tempered as Mark. Though we are convinced that Mark is an achiever who will pursue a successful career, we remain firm in the belief that Adrian will continue to be 'chained to a middle-class complacency' that turns hopes and aspirations to nought. Sadly, in spite of the author's best intentions, Mark's accomplishments are not likely to brighten the bourgeois world of Selvon's most pessimistic novel.

In both middle-class novels, Selvon presents contrasting pictures of the world to which he belonged socially and intellectually. Though Selvon himself confessed to enjoying Carnival, his enjoyment was never extreme as that of Mark and Adrian; though he jumped with the bands, he never found the need to 'play mas'. If all Trinidadian middle-class citizens were cast in Adrian's mould, there would be little chance of social and political progress; though it is true that many uncannily resemble Adrian, it is also true that

many, through commitment and diligence, continue to enhance the overall quality of island life. Andrews, Hope and
Foster, in their moderation, balance and patriotism provide a
necessary counterbalance to the excessive self-interest of
Adrian and Randolph and the craven dereliction of Johnny.

THE IMMIGRANT NOVELS

The Housing Lark is Selvon's second immigrant novel; surprisingly it does not continue the Moses narrative since the
character of his most famous immigrant had stirred some nine
years before the imagination of readers who no doubt eagerly
wanted to read of the further picaresque adventures of Moses
and 'the boys' in London. *The Housing Lark* is unique among
the immigrant novels in several ways: it advocates marriage as
the answer to many immigrant problems; its primary concern
is the ubiquitous housing problem faced by immigrants; it
exploits humour for its own sake; and it establishes the
superiority of the immigrant woman over her male counter-
part. This is a novel that celebrates the significant part that
women played in the evolution and amelioration of immigrant
life; it therefore serves as a necessary balance to the largely
masculine narrative of Moses and 'the boys'.[4]

Harry Banjo, a Jamaican calypsonian, casually broaches the
'idea' of the boys' owning their own house; it naturally takes
root in the immigrant psyche, although it is not treated with
the seriousness that it deserves. To 'the boys' and the anonymous male narrator, the idea is doomed to fail because it
emerges in summer, when they would rather spend their
money on the erotic pleasures offered by the glorious season.
It is to them merely a 'lark'; but to the women it is serious
business. To them, it is not simply a matter of not having to
pay rent; more importantly, ownership means security, pride
and new sense of identity.

The Housing Lark is Selvon's most obtrusively comic novel,
seemingly constructed to provoke laughter for its own sake. In
this novel, more than in any other, Selvon bridges the gap
between native orality and the scribal tradition; more so than
The Lonely Londoners, it is essentially an oral performance

which assumes the form of a scribal presentation. It explores and exploits the risible, establishing humour as a moral mode of sorts in the immigrant experience as it is in the home-based Caribbean experience. Humour is the island-forged weapon, annealed in the fires of slavery, indenture and genocide, which the immigrant instinctively wields against the chimeras of an alienating culture; it is the innate resilience against the vicissitudes of white superiority. As ubiquitous and ineradicable as the native nutgrass, it manifests itself in *The Housing Lark* in several forms: situational (Syl outfoxes Ram for hard-to-find accommodation); dialogic (Jean's explanation to Harry of what she does); imaginary (Battersby fantasizes that by rubbing the wallpaper lamp, the genie will appear to provide money, food, rum and women); fortuitous (Harry's unfair incarceration works in his favour as it boosts his career as a recording artist); linguistic (the plethora of such deliberate creations as 'pennycitis', 'belging' and 'patty-the-four grass', among others); and cultural (the narrator's indulgent description of the West Indian irresistible proclivity to toy with and manipulate language). The West Indian male is more often than not a man of infinite jest. Humour is the salient strategy through which the Caribbean, unique among outposts of the empire because it is the first region where so many races were brought together, speaks and writes back. The commingling of Amerindian, African, Indian, Chinese, Portuguese, Syrian, French, Spanish and English cultural traditions, among others, afforded the West Indian access to a linguistic hodgepodge of incredible vitality and opulence. His experience of protracted colonial servitude initially rendered him inarticulate; eventually, his reliance on native sources and access to a variety of other traditions created a response to his tragic circumstances. This response is characterized by humour, that ability to see and imagine the silver lining of the most ominous cloud. Without humour, immigrant life is simply unimaginable and intolerable. It is, as Selvon demonstrates especially in the immigrant novels, the defining shibboleth of Caribbean peoples.

Battersby, the self-appointed treasurer of the housing lark, in total disregard, spends what he collects; the boys renege on their promise to stop smoking and drinking; and they carry on their merry way with no real commitment. Matilda, with more thought than Harry Banjo, remembers an indelible part of her native island experience and proposes the 'idea' of the excursion to Hampton Court; the boys, always ready for fun and excitement, make it possible. The excursion becomes the perfect vehicle for showcasing the nature of West Indian humour; Selvon carefully keeps this fictive excursion close to the ritual island outings (as they were commonly called in Selvon's day). Because humour is his primary objective, Selvon exaggerates somewhat the frenetic activity on the bus; however, the drinking, eating, the repartees, the reproof of children by chattering adults, the clatter of pots and pans, the knocking of bottle and spoon, and the movement of feet in time to calypso music, are authentic. Having alighted at their destination, men, women and children displaying little restraint, yet mindful of where they are, transform a riparian scene on the Thames, the most famous of rivers, into an immigrant version of a typical Trinidad river lime at Caura or Valencia, nestling in the Northern Range.[5] These immigrants have irrepressibly superimposed in their inimitable fashion on the staid, stolid culture of the British, their rollicking island customs, the best example of which is the Notting Hill Carnival.

With all its problems, the excursion is a financial success; it is also an impressive tour de force on Selvon's part. Nowhere else in his fiction do we find such a compelling and graphic depiction of immigrant life in all its natural exuberance. The success of the excursion encourages Teena, Selvon's heroine, to insist on 'a day of reckoning' when she demands that Battersby reveal all the money he has been given. She takes complete charge, delivering 'a pep talk' which transforms the 'liars and renegades' into husbands who understand the value and implications of owning a house. Both men and women can look forward to a new sense of identity, to a rise, however small, in pride of ownership, to a novel grasp of the value of family life, and to an overall appreciable improvement to immigrant life. In *The Housing Lark*, Selvon presents the brighter, lighter, more comic side of immigrant life in a grim and lonely London.

The Lonely Londoners is Selvon's third novel and his first immigrant novel, coming after a peasant novel and a middle-class novel. Consequently, it differs from both island-based works; it depicts the life of the West Indian immigrant, lured to London by the inverse El Dorado myth (that the city streets are paved with gold), and it underscores Moses's (and Selvon's) need to leave the green Caribbean for anticipated brighter fortunes. It describes the struggle of the immigrant in the 1940s and 1950s against grim winters, racial discrimination, hunger, inhuman accommodation and a soul-destroying deracination in an alien city. Conversely, it celebrates the resilience of the working-class West Indian male, who seeks refuge and solace in the release of summer, in easy, casual sex with white women and in the regular Sunday-morning gatherings in Moses's dingy basement room. *The Lonely Londoners* is a tribute to the pragmatism, optimism and character of the West Indian immigrant in an ambivalent culture that both invites and repels him.

The triumph of *The Lonely Londoners* is Selvon's deliberate choice of an unorthodox structure, narrative strategy and linguistic medium. The narrative comprises eight divided sections (episode, ballad, flashback, reflection, confession, explanation, musing and philosophy) held together by the consciousness of a third-person narrator, who sometimes merges with Selvon and Moses, other times distances himself from both. The achronological structure narrates key moments in the life of Moses Aloetta, partly a fictional version of Eric Busby, one of the first wave of West Indian immigrants in the 1940s who eventually returned to Trinidad. The conversational tone, the dramatic immediacy, the use of Trinidad dialect, the humour, and especially the pathos contribute to giving form and substance to what may be considered the archetypal immigrant novel, whose primary aim is to establish the remarkable ability of the immigrant to fashion strategies to cope with the adversities, challenges, and anxieties of living with little sense of belonging in 'the great city'.

After working almost 13 years in a factory that manufactures pot scourers, Moses is unable to save any money; basic needs use up his meagre wages. He is unable to move from his cramped, dirty basement room with 'a leaky skylight'. Whatever mobility he enjoys is of the most banal kind; he experiences a financial, emotional, social stasis, which forces him to confess, 'I ain't get no place at all, I still in the same way, neither forward nor backward'. As the dire rigours of winter compel him to contemplate returning to the 'green islands', so the erotic pleasures of summer inveigle him to postpone his return indefinitely. Though the warmth and laxities of island life constantly call to him, the sense of history and romance felt everywhere in London keeps him in a city, where the sun seems a 'force-ripe orange', where 'half-past ten in the morning' looks like 'seven in the evening' and the back of the railway station is 'another world' and 'look[s] like hell'.

When Henry Oliver arrives at Waterloo Station in the dead of winter he intrigues Moses by wearing a tropical suit, having no baggage, no rum and little money. Marvelling at the arrival's feigned insouciance, Moses instinctively feels compassion for him, taking him in, feeding him and enjoying his company. In typical Trinidadian style, he christens him Sir Galahad, no doubt because there is to Moses something far more fictional than real about the droll adventurer. Guided by Selvon, who will pick up the imagery at the very end of the trilogy, Moses sends this seemingly fearless young man on a grail quest in a city where love, chastity, chalice and God are conspicuously absent. It is Galahad's natural question that provides Moses and Selvon with an opportunity to tell of his metropolitan experience: 'If things bad like that how come you still holding on in Brit'n?' Moses's rapturous description of the heady delights of 'summer is hearts' provides the real answer, though nowhere Moses confesses it. Perhaps Moses lacks the candour and veracity to answer Galahad's pivotal question directly; perhaps Selvon has not given Moses a sufficiently profound understanding of his metropolitan experience to provide him with the answer.

Selvon, remembering his presentation of his first hero, characterizes Moses as a representative yet atypical immigrant, a choric repository of black immigrant experience. He is the conscience of his immigrant fraternity, sharing their regular woes and rare moments of pleasure, yet he is the only one burdened and privileged by reflection, musing and contemplation. Tiger is Selvon's thinking peasant; Moses is his thinking immigrant, although his intellectual accomplishments are puny compared to Tiger's impressive literacy. Yet, he is given a larger compassion and sympathy than his peasant counter-part. Always at Waterloo Station to greet and view arrivals, Moses instinctively sees himself in every one who steps off the boat train, feeling 'a great compassion for every one of them, as if he live each of their lives, one by one' and internalizing their 'strain and stress'. With little thought of the future, he oscillates between the past and the present, shuttling back and forth like the London fog that prevents looking ahead with clarity. His years of exile at the heart of the empire have made him the recognized leader of his immigrant community; he is a 'welfare officer', a 'liaison officer', an adviser, friend and mentor to his constituents. In providing a meeting-place for the boys 'every Sunday morning, like if they going to church', Moses may be seen as the pastor of the London Immigrant Church of the Metropolitan Faith. In a godless city, where weather forecasters have replaced the prophets of old, Moses's message is purely secular as the boys congregate for 'old talk, to find out the latest gen, what happening, where is the next fete . . .' Choosing his text from his immigrant experience, he homilizes to his captive congregation on why 'life really hard for the boys . . . in a lonely miserable city'. The absence of religion in the West Indian immigrant, especially among the women, is a measure of the soul-destroying nature of the London experience, for religious belief is a determinant in everyday life as powerful as any in the Caribbean.

Though Moses is without a family, without love, without savings, without a sense of achievement, he is not without hope. Not eminently successful, Moses has cleared in his inimitable manner every barrier the host culture has erected to prevent his social mobility. For his stamina, his resilience and his compassion, he is rewarded with a moment of privilege that easily stands out from all others in the immigrant novels. Though he does not display any literary talent or aspiration (helping Lewis to write a letter of apology to his wife hardly counts for anything), he stands on the banks of the Thames, contemplating the contradictory nature of immigrant experi-ence, filled with 'misery and pathos' wondering 'if he could ever write a book . . . What everybody would buy'. The resonance of this unique moment takes us by surprise for nothing prepares us for this revelation. To be sure, Moses's experience is the true stuff of fiction, but Moses cannot know this; his ideal retirement is an artless one, of lying in the sun, eating fish broth, talking to fishermen and sleeping all day long under a tree (*LL* 114). As Selvon had stepped in at the beginning of the narrative to give Moses a 'good chance to say his mind', so too at the end he intervenes to give what he gives to Balgobin, 'his glorious episode of history'. Moses, without his best seller, has all the credentials to become the hero of the oral history of 'the boys' in London; Moses, the author of his metropolitan memoirs, like Selvon, will become a household name and chronicler to generations. Ultimately, Selvon wisely leaves Moses with a more characteristic and credible musing of how on such a night the absence of sex makes the lonely Londoner even lonelier. We take final leave of Moses the philanderer and Moses the would-be author.

Some 19 years later, Selvon resumes the Moses narrative, moving forward into the 1970s, when the Black Power movement is gathering steam and illegal immigration is on the rise. The impecunious Moses of *The Lonely Londoners* has saved enough to purchase his own terrace, even if it is one that is carded for 'LCC demolition'. Moses confesses at the beginning of *Moses Ascending* that he is 'on the lookout for an investment in truth'; of the two meanings of the phrase, the Trinidadian (really on the lookout for an investment) is the one that immediately comes to mind. The other standard meaning, however, when applied to the entire narrative, indicates the depth of Selvon's irony and censure. Hardly the investment he anticipated, Moses's purchase turns out to be an exercise in deception, lies, illegality and promiscuity. With his purchase, Moses changes his status from tenant to landlord and leaves the all-too-familiar squalor of his dingy basement room in Bayswater for the cleaner ambience of a penthouse in Shepherd's Bush. To bolster and confirm his new status, he hires as his 'man Friday a white immigrant from somewhere in the Midlands' who attends to the petty details of running the house.

Monetarily and socially, then, Moses has done remarkably well; there is, however, no corresponding moral elevation, although there is some attempt at literary accomplishment. With time on his hands, Moses, with all credit due to him, decides to write his memoirs. On the surface this is as laudable as Moses's 'wondering' at the end of *The Lonely Londoners*; unfortunately, Moses does not understand what the writing of memoirs entails. Rather than reflecting on lived experience, establishing meaningful patterns, and exploiting key moments, a preposterous Moses goes in search of material for his 'magnus opus'. Of course, this is Selvon's way of telling us that he has lost admiration and sympathy for the character that won his approbation two decades before. Moses, not surprisingly, never completes his memoirs; his inability to achieve his objective is a measure of his failure as a protagonist and a man. Our recollection of what it is to be a man for Tiger permits us to understand the chasm that separates peasant hero from immigrant fool. Whatever of the memoirs is completed in first draft is severely censured by Brenda, a representative intellectual of the new generation of black Britons; her criticism, though superficial and merely grammatical, emphasizes the level of Moses's self-deception. His instinctive method of composition resembles that of Selvon, who confesses that he never learned the formal rules of writing; however, Moses's lack of success is in marked contrast to Selvon's singular achievements. Galahad, who cannot lay claim to any significant intellectual accomplishment, is much more to the point, and is manipulated by Selvon to make fun of his friend: 'You tackling something what you don't know one arse about.' Such a criticism indicates that Galahad has turned the tables on Moses: Moses of *The Lonely Londoners* is the veteran, guiding and advising all his fellow immigrants; in the sequel, Moses merely pretends to be in charge. Selvon and such characters as Bob, Jeannie, Brenda, Faizul and Galahad manipulate him at will. Moses has been reduced to a pathetic figure, a ghost of man, as venal as he is lustful, incapable of controlling the illegal trafficking of immigrants in his building and of withstanding the simple-minded overtures of Jeannie and the sexual bravado of Brenda.

Brenda's involvement in and dedication to the party are laudable; but her lack of sexual scruples cannot augur well for her generation of mobile blacks. Her physical beauty, her education and sophistication count for little in Selvon's darkening satire of immigrant mentality and behaviour. She is no different in sexual behaviour from the major players in the narrative: Bob, Jeannie and Moses. Selvon creates in *Moses Ascending* a moral world in which few if any rules inhere; the punishment for sexual infidelity is treated with a lightness that renders it almost innocent. Brenda is actually rewarded for her sexual escapades with Bob and Moses, Jeannie is treated with kid gloves, Bob gains the upper hand in his sexual competition with Moses, while Moses loses both his penthouse and credibility. Selvon creates a narrative to illustrate Moses's susceptibility to deception by self and other; he is the greatest loser of all. Whereas Brenda and Galahad are fiercely committed to the Party and what it means for the advancement of black consciousness, Moses turns his back on his own, content only to make money and to continue composing his ludicrously conceived memoirs.

Both Selvon and Moses, it appears, become jaded: Moses consciously transforms himself into an 'Oreo gentleman' despising his fellow Blacks and what they represent, though he has recently discovered the joys of having sex with a black woman. Within his crusty black exterior lies a mushy imitation of a white gentleman; he is, in Selvon's words, a 'whitewashed black man', capable only of vacuous mimicry. Selvon, too, after two and a half decades in London grows irritable, impatient and cynical; he senses the need for a change, for new challenges. His deprecation of Moses is as deliberate as it is scathing; he can no longer accord his protagonist (now transformed into an anti-hero) his approbation nor his sympathy. At the end of *The Lonely Londoners*, and on occasion during the narrative, Selvon and Moses work together to endow the veteran immigrant with an earned respectability and a chastened, reflective wisdom. Throughout *Moses Ascending*, however, Selvon, at dire odds with his protagonist, relentlessly manipulates him from one self-demeaning episode to the next. At the end of *Moses Ascending* we feel as we feel at the end of *I Hear Thunder*: men and women, caught in a sensual music, have lost their way, as money, power and expediency become lodestars; such time-tested virtues as truth, loyalty and integrity have been overwhelmed by an overarching lubricity. We take leave of a lust-wearied, sexually immature Moses planning to apprise Jeannie of Bob's sexual indiscretions with

Brenda so that he can resume his philandering with his batman's all-too-willing wife. If Selvon had initially wanted simply to make fun of a black man who would rather be white, for some reason he changes his mind and launches into a relentless satire against a contemptible, morally flaccid Moses.

Moses Migrating is Selvon's last novel, and the third and final narrative in the Moses saga; Selvon did not contemplate any further continuation. Of the narratives that comprise the trilogy, the last is the darkest: approbation and sympathy pale into censure, humour is replaced by cynicism, and irony and sarcasm give way to incremental satire. In both *The Lonely Londoners* and *Moses Ascending*, Moses can justifiably boast of achievement, modest as it is; in *Moses Migrating*, however, there is boasting but no achievement. Having grown tired of his protagonist, Selvon allows him to continue to make a consummate ass of himself. After four decades in London, Moses returns to the land of his birth; after forty years in the 'great City' Moses has superficially transformed himself into one of England's black gentry. He wears the appropriate clothes, adopts, as far as his minimal education allows, the requisite speech, and generally apes the manners and physical comportment of the English gentleman. The characterization of the Moses of *Moses Migrating*, more so than that of *Moses Ascending*, is a study in self-deception and wanton mimicry. If handsome is as handsome does (*MM* 34), then Moses as he concludes his narrative is ugly indeed.

Returning eventually to Trinidad offers Moses a chance of a lifetime for meaningful reformation. This is an opportunity to reconnect with his true self, to touch the native pulse and to show the wisdom and maturity the many years in the heart of the empire have brought him. After the rise and fall in *Moses Ascending*, Selvon offers him a chance to put behind once and for all the hustling, the restlessness, the emptiness and the sexual indulgence. Tanty Flora (a name redolent of nature and nurture), who raised Moses as an orphan into adulthood, has reared another waif, Doris (from the Greek meaning 'gift'), a chaste, beautiful, and self-assured woman. Tanty brings her two charges together, virtually gifting Doris to the visitor; the meeting instantly bears fruit as both fall in love with each other. Love is a new emotion for both lovers though they are worlds apart: Doris is a virgin, looking for a husband to take her away to a better life; Moses, a chronic philanderer who has never considered taking a wife. Almost magically these two markedly opposite individuals are given a chance to transform their humdrum lives. Doris does all that she can to show Moses that she loves him though she never confesses that she does; Moses does everything to repudiate the love that he so insistently and glibly declares.

After enjoying J'Ouvert with him, Doris reluctantly gives herself to Moses, though she confesses that she enjoyed having sex with him. Moses, a creature of habit, virtually forces himself on a protesting Doris, though she has placed herself, tired on his hotel bed, in a vulnerable position. Moses, the professed lover instinctively yields to Moses, the unrestrained rake, who deflowers the young woman; to him the beautiful, chaste, highly desirable Doris becomes simply another sexual conquest. The native manicou cannot change its scavenger habits; Moses programmed and moulded by his immigrant experience, treats Doris worse than the 'dilapidated sleeper' of his Bayswater days. Selvon does not permit Moses after the hotel incident an opportunity to explain why he does not commit himself to Doris, who neither resents nor chastises her lover. We are therefore left to deduce that Moses, who no doubt feels a new emotion never encountered in all his years in London, is unable or afraid to surrender to it. His metropolitan years has enured him to sex without love, have made him a misogynistic automaton, a man for whom every woman, regardless of individual credentials, is a sexual plaything.

Moses completes two nostoi in *Moses Migrating*: one back to Trinidad, the land of his birth, and the other back to London, his adoptive homeland. The former brings him the immense self-satisfaction of winning the silver cup for best individual masquerader; the other, only the uncertainty of being allowed into Britain as a returning immigrant. Selvon's mordant irony cuts a wide swath: Moses, in appointing himself Her Majesty's ambassador and in playing Britannia as his masquerade, concretizes his unwavering support for and belief in the supremacy of a culture that has placed so many barriers between him and self-actualization. Moses's cruel abandonment of Doris and his implacable faith in all that England has to offer make him 'a composite man among mimic men'. These are Brenda's words in the narrative; they are as well Selvon's final assessment of the older immigrant, stuck in a time warp, who has turned his back on the vision and struggle of the new generation of black Britons for acceptance and equality in a culture that is resistant to change. The final phrase of the novel, '. . . I was still playing charades' with its emphasis on silly pretence and playing games, nicely delineates the characterization of the Moses of *Moses Ascending* and of *Moses Migrating*. For the former, acquiring a terrace is the rationalization of selfish mimicry; for the latter, carnival is a metaphor for his penchant for masquerading and his inability to present his true face or authentic self.

Moses's fantasy that the silver cup is the Holy Grail serves at least two functions: one, it takes us back some 27 years to his christening of Henry Oliver as Sir Galahad; neither the later Moses nor Galahad is afforded any reformative vision to transform their lives into exemplars of chastity and devotion to an ideal. They resemble more an effete Sir Lancelot, whose inability to rein his illicit passion destroys the integrity and limitless possibilities of Camelot. Additionally, it indicates the chasm that separates adult responsibility with its tests and travails from an immature masquerading, in which the jaundiced mind twists reality into a variety of comforting illusions. Unlike the legendary Galahad and his biblical namesake, Moses lacks the moral wisdom, fidelity to a cause and the transcendent will to achieve any measure of heroism. He remains at the end of the trilogy a pathetic anti-hero, who has failed to maximize the opportunities life has offered him. In Selvon's fictional world, this is tantamount to self-condemnation.

The Moses trilogy works quite differently from the cane trilogy; the latter depicts the peasants' ability to overcome all the barriers history and political conquest have erected in their way, as one perfects the cane cutter's art (Balgobin), another learns as much about cane as he can (Babolal), another insists on pulling himself out of the quagmire of ignorance and illiteracy and grasps the value of becoming politically involved (Tiger) and another understands in a plural society the need for creolization and a university education (Romesh). The cane

trilogy depicts the apotheosis of the Indo-Trinidadian peasantry, whose indomitable struggle and sometimes ambivalent
faith in the future are endorsed and approved of by Selvon.
The Moses trilogy, by contrast, is a study in deprecation and
diminution, from the reflection and contemplation of writing a
best seller to the absurdity of writing memoirs in total
ignorance of what they entail, to the unabashed endorsement
of the supremacy of British culture and becoming the mimic
man par excellence. Unlike the peasant, Moses has not really
lived; he has merely survived. Whatever modicum of achievement can be attributed to Moses in *Moses Ascending* and *Moses
Migrating* is nullified by the simpleton figure who woefully
and consciously deceives himself into believing that he has
achieved something by being a competent masquerader and
that Britain, unaware of his wretched existence, will reward
him for his stout support of her. The peasant has fought the
good fight and possesses all the qualities requisite for un-
limited success; the privative immigrant has maundered from
episode to episode, gleaning little wisdom to take him into a
future of promise.

Though we cannot change the order in which they were
written and published, we can, if we wanted a balance to the
cane trilogy, reorder the Moses narratives. In this reordering,
Moses Ascending would come first, followed by *Moses Migrating*, with *The Lonely Londoners* as the final narrative. This
reordering then would present the story of Moses who, after
some time in London, saves enough to purchase a terrace. His
time as a landlord has brought him a sense of achievement and
wealth empowering him to return to his native land, where he
meets, loves and deserts the finest woman he has ever known.
After carnival, during which he wins a silver cup for masquerading as Britannia, he returns to Britain to reflect on his years
in London and to contemplate turning his metropolitan experience into a best seller. If we take leave of Moses at this point,
we can establish the apotheosis of the immigrant. When we
consider that Selvon is as much a character as he is author and
narrator, we are encouraged to believe that he would approve
of such a recasting of his triptych. This of course is pure
surmise, poetic licence, as it were.

Conclusion

Selvon's short fiction and novels have earned him a unique place in West Indian literature; his achievements and contributions are as substantial as they are crucial. He is widely credited with providing the catalyst for the renaissance of West Indian literature; before 1952, there was no body of poems, short stories, and novels recognizable as West Indian literature. While novels by James, Reid and Mittelholzer, among others, had stirred the imagination of readers and critics, none had the dramatic and enormous impact of *A Brighter Sun*. With the publication of Selvon's first novel, West Indian literature with its defining concerns, settings, and accents finally emerged from the protracted doldrums, receiving the boost it so desperately needed to make it a legitimate member of the family of literatures written in English. Selvon's first three novels ushered in the golden age of West Indian literature, defined by the brilliance of Naipaul, Harris and Walcott, among many others.

It was Selvon's cogent depiction of various aspects of the Trinidadian landscape, his risky but calculated use of dialect, and his deliberate characterization of Tiger as a peasant with an atypical drive to overcome ignorance and illiteracy that struck a new note, endearing foreign and local readers to his fictional world. Its verisimilitude and authenticity compelled foreign critics to take notice of what was happening in the literature of this unique region of the empire. The teaching of such mainstream authors as Chaucer, Shakespeare, Defoe, Hardy, Dickens, and especially Wordsworth, over a century, no doubt created in West Indian writers the need to do for their culture what the English poets and novelists did for theirs. The English countryside and its flora and fauna were naturally replaced by a recognizable Caribbean setting of mountains, rivers, forests and indigenous trees and flowers (moor, oak, and daffodil yielded to canefield, samaan, and hibiscus); farm hands, shepherds and grain-field workers, too, were supplanted by cane-cutters, unschooled peasants, and a working class, desperate to shake off the yoke of slavery and indenture. Dickens and Hardy had successfully employed the dialect of the working class, the criminal and the peasant; Selvon followed their lead by consciously allowing Tiger, Joe, Urmilla and Moses to be their authentic selves, to express their experience in a peculiar demeanour and in the only language they know, a dialect with its peculiar grammatical rules, a penchant for the racy and humorous, and a lexicon that borrows freely from many linguistic traditions.

The significance of Selvon's deliberate glorification of the working class has won him the accolade of the greatest folk poet the West Indies has produced; no one would seriously disagree with Lamming's well-known assessment. In his understanding of Wordsworth's theoretical democratization and practice of poetry, Selvon undoubtedly grasped the enormous literary possibilities of humble, ordinary folk. What the romantic poet did for the leech gatherer, the village beggar, shepherd and vagrant mother, Selvon does for the peasant (Tiger, Sarojini, Balgobin), the working-class individual (Moses, Joe, Ma Lambie), and the social pariah (More Lazy, Soylo and Manko). Both writers invest their characters with a humanity and dignity denied to them by society at large; like Wordsworth, Selvon understands that each individual, no matter how downtrodden and marginalized, has his own peculiar counter-narrative, so crucial in effecting a necessary democratic balance, as he clearly indicates in early non-fiction piece, 'Ralph Will Try Again': 'A chap like Ralph you would never look at twice, but he – as the rest of us – has a story to tell' (*FM* 55). In his fictional treatment of the ordinary man, Selvon created a broad and rewarding path which West Indian novelists eagerly followed: Lovelace, Khan, Clarke, among so many others, have acknowledged their debt to him. Surely, without Selvon's lead, Naipaul's early works would have been different, for they quite obviously capitalize on his groundbreaking efforts.

With his primary objective of putting Trinidad on the literary map, Selvon set out to present in his fiction a personal interpretation of the narratives of three disparate communities: the Indo-Trinidadian peasantry, the Afro-West Indian immigrant working class in London, and middle-class Trinidadians, separated by historical circumstances, ethnic traditions and rituals, and values. Though socially not of their class, Selvon is able to enter the experience of the Hindu peasants sufficiently to convince us that his portraits of peasant characters are recognizable and real, endowing his characters with verisimilitude, that literary quality so highly prized by Coleridge and his contemporaries. So successful is Selvon that we, middle-class readers, readily identify with Tiger's quest for knowledge, admiring and endorsing his unrelenting drive to pull himself out of the quicksand of ignorance and illiteracy. Unlike Mittelholzer, who is content to portray in *Corentyne Thunder* (1941) his 16-year-old peasant heroine, Kattree, as merely a person of complacent emotions, Selvon wisely and courageously invests his 16-year-old peasant hero with his own middle-class interest in increasing knowledge and his belief in and commitment to the creative process. This makes Tiger atypical; yet his love for the land, for gardening and for hard manual labour establishes him as representative of his kind. This seeming contradiction is a function of Selvon's need to use Tiger as a vehicle for his presentation of the evolution of the Hindu peasant, who moves from cutting cane, to gardening, to graduating from university, to becoming a professional, and part of management. His cane trilogy – *A Brighter Sun, Turn Again Tiger* and *The Plains of Caroni* – celebrates the struggle of the Hindu peasant for acceptance and success in a creolized world. No other writer has devoted so much energy to depicting the coming of age of the Hindu peasant, struggling from the abject squalor of the barracks, to the comfort – often ostentatious – of individual homes, to insistence on the inestimable value of education and schooling and to significant participation in the political process. Selvon's first three peasant novels comprise the only epic in West Indian literature of the heroic ordeal of the Indo-Trinidadian peasantry; in fictional terms, an odyssey from strenuous toil in canefields and gardens to becoming a professional part of management;

in socio-political terms, the courageous journey from canefield worker to prime minister.

Selvon, in his Moses trilogy, *The Lonely Londoners*, *Moses Ascending* and *Moses Migrating*, no doubt initially thought of doing for the Afro-West Indian immigrant what he does for the Indo-Trinidadian peasant in the cane trilogy. Initially, because there is a symmetry of sorts between *A Brighter Sun* and *The Lonely Londoners*: both working-class protagonists (gardener and factory worker) struggle against tremendous odds for identity, respectability and social mobility; both become leaders of their respective fraternities, becoming confidant, advisor and mentor; both display admirable resilience and perseverance; and both come to recognize the value of turning their defining experience into art. Though the differences between both works are more telling than the similarities, this consonance is more than superficial; it is an indication of Selvon's original intentions. Given his early cosmopolitanism in San Fernando, and his lifelong belief in the need for a proper understanding of creolization, Selvon felt equally at home with Indo-Trinidadians and Afro-Trinidadians; he proudly boasts in interviews of belonging to a 'third race', to use his own phrase. In his drive to put Trinidad on the map through his writing, he saw the opportunity to exert his literary energies in creating what is the fullest Trinidadian canvas in West Indian literature by giving equal space and importance to the island's two largest ethnic groups.

The completion of *The Lonely Londoners*, however, given that it ends on a surprisingly privileged note, did not allow him to continue the Moses narrative to the apotheosis of the West Indian immigrant. For nothing in *The Lonely Londoners* reveals that Moses is even vaguely interested in turning his London experience into a best-seller; continuing the narrative to the writing of this imagined volume and beyond would have been too serious a task. Selvon's penchant for humour, his grasp of its role in immigrant experience and his growing enui with London and his need to emigrate were crucial factors in his execution of the two last novels of his trilogy of diminution. We see gentle humour and engaging pathos metamorphose into biting satire that still makes us laugh, this time not with Moses but at him. Selvon's increasing use of expletives indicates his anger towards Moses and his impatience and frustration with life in London. So when Moses describes himself as 'a wet cunt of the first water' (*MA* 128) he causes us to laugh at the fresh way of stating a rare confession; it is the juxtaposition of 'wet' and 'water' with its suggestion of sexual readiness, the reduction of Brenda, Jeannie and himself to an anatomical area, and his lack of understanding of the implications of his self-censure that bring more than a smile or blush to our faces. While the peasant picture grows in colour, achievement and optimism, the immigrant canvas darkens, and fades into buffoonery, self-deprecation and satire. Tiger, Romesh and Sarojini – Selvon's composite peasant – represent the apotheosis of the Hindu peasant; the Moses of the two later narratives represents the utter diminishment of the immigrant protagonist.

We may choose to avoid or write off *Moses Ascending* and *Moses Migrating* as curious and inappropriate; we cannot, however, fail to appreciate Selvon's approbation of Moses's struggle in *The Lonely Londoners*. Though there are inadequacies in Moses's character – complacency, inability to save money as the Jamaicans do, sexual indulgence, an altogether worldly and materialistic outlook – there are compensatory strengths: a broad, deep sympathy for fellow immigrants, an understanding of their needs, the ability to muse and reflect on life, and the feeling at the very end that he could translate his years of exile into an exemplary narrative. This is the Moses we choose to remember and carry with us: the archetypal West Indian immigrant, who is invested with a fair portion of his author's metropolitan experience and his belief in the value of creative fiction. Tiger and Moses are in different ways representative peasant and immigrant respectively, made atypical and unique by their interest in the possibilities of art.

Selvon's presentation of the island bourgeois world is at best ambivalent. *An Island is a World* is his most serious novel, and confessedly, his favourite. In contrast, *I Hear Thunder*, his second middle-class novel, is his least successful narrative. In the former, the major characters, Andrews, Hope and Foster, form a triumvirate who work together in different ways to enhance the social and political condition of the island. Their frequent meetings are opportunities for Selvon to give insights into the intellectual (Foster), religious (Hope) and political

(Andrews) life of Trinidad in the 1940s. While Hope does not marry, Andrews and Foster choose wives whose commitment to and belief in their husbands become the foundation on which they build separate careers; marriage, as in *The Housing Lark*, is a serious and necessary social institution in this fictional world. In *I Hear Thunder*, however, there is little that is serious; Selvon, it seems, writes the novel to show the other and less attractive side of the bourgeois coin. Here, men and women move along the surfaces of things, finding greater meaning in the bacchanalian abandon of carnival than in any attempt to improve the quality of island life. Adrian's self-imposed sexual abstinence proves a vacuous penance for his chronic over-indulgence; Randolph's hypochondria and obsessional anxiety with sexual performance is an index of the 'drowsy complacency' of his world; Polly's and Joyce's easy seductions indicate their inability to rise above the sexual and the trite; and Mark's interest in running for political office appears to be a desperate attempt to find true meaning in his life, a substitute for any sincere sexual feeling for his weak wife. In this potboiler, Randolph, Mark and Adrian comprise Selvon's composite Trinidadian bourgeois character: a combination of professionalism and sexual over-indulgence, in which the latter overwhelms the former. While we know that Selvon endorses the life and struggle of Hope, Foster and Andrews, we are hard-pressed to find any moral endorsement of the lives of his major characters in *I Hear Thunder*. Mark is a good man, a caring son and successful professional, yet he displays an unrealistic nonchalance and acceptance of his wife's infidelity with his best friend.

The other paramount contribution Selvon makes to West Indian literature is his deliberate use of the Trinidadian linguistic continuum. It is worth noting that, although Selvon brings together Jamaicans, Barbadians, Grenadians, Dominicans, Vincentians and Trinidadians together in his fiction, he consciously makes them speak a distinctively Trinidadian dialect, some of it not immediately intelligible to non-Trinidadians and to Trinidadians of a later generation. Take, for example, these words taken from 'Come Back to Grenada', '. . . with byayr and buicken and buttards one, and talaline farts' which come from the once ubiquitous game of marbles.

Of the dozens of Trinidadians I have approached, most have never heard the phrase 'with byayr and buicken' and no one has explained it satisfactorily; there are, too, conflicting interpretations of 'talaline'. This anomaly evidently has bothered no one, as there has been no questioning in Selvon criticism of the authenticity of accented regional dialects.

In all his poems except the last he employs Trinidadian standard, the language regularly used by educated Trinidadians. This is the language too he uses for narration and description in the majority of early short fictional pieces and in all his novels except the immigrant novels. In these four immigrant novels Selvon uses the everyday speech of the uneducated, non-professional Trinidadian. This is a dialect that shows contempt for standard grammar, accepted word order, normal inflexions and recognizable vocabulary. In some ways, it is more natural and authentic than standard; consequently, it is also used voluntarily by educated islanders for a variety of practical reasons and effects: for emphasis, candour, humour, for pride in being a Trinidadian, and for being one of the boys. Only pedantic despisers of the vernacular religiously avoid using it. Even Naipaul, who has covered his Trinidadian lilt and cadence with an Oxford patina, can slip into the vernacular when necessary, as we learn in a wonderfully humorous episode with Selvon and Ken Ramchand in his authorized biography, *The World Is What It Is* (455–6). Though Trinidad standard is the language of parliament, almost every speaker increasingly feels the need to use the vernacular for special effect, especially to hurl 'picong' (good-natured banter with a sting to it) at a member across the floor. It is not far-fetched to suggest that Selvon, in his deliberate and fearless use of the vernacular, shows the way for parliamentarians and others.

Before *The Lonely Londoners*, Selvon employs standard English for narration and description and the vernacular in dialogue; in *A Brighter Sun* he introduced readers to a variety of creole and Hindi/Bhojpuri phrases, as he illustrates Tiger's struggle to come to terms with and to master the language of books. In his first immigrant novel, Selvon amplifies this urge to be authentic, lyrical and faithful to his island roots. He never lost faith in the richness of Trinidadian vernacular; proleptically, he speaks of its 'poetic

101

power, the imagery and vividness' and muses on 'how tremendous are the literary possibilities of our dialect' (SC no. 89). Having attempted many times to write the first Moses narrative in standard English and failed, he yielded to his instincts and used the language of the uneducated Trinidadian. The narrative began to flow, and, as Selvon says in several interviews, it came naturally and easily to him, and 'wrote itself' in six months. Not quite automatic writing, it nevertheless has the unmistakable salt and tang of the spoken dialect with a cogent authenticity: no other register would be appropriate for Moses and the boys. Though the episodic tale lacks the ordonnance of the traditional novel, it marks a significant watershed in the development of West Indian narrative. It is the first work to employ the vernacular as the language of narration, description, dialogue, reminiscence, musing and philosophizing. It represents a triumphant moment of linguistic manumission for West Indians, emancipating them from the shackled restraint of the language of the colonial master, and giving them a fresh sense of the true capability and versatility of a dialect, too long deprecated and vilified by teachers and other professionals. *The Lonely Londoners* may be the most important of West Indian novels, as central to an understanding of the evolution of West Indian narrative as any other. It is a glorious celebration of the suppleness, versatility and plenitude of the everyday language of Trinidadians, the apotheosis, as it were, of the vernacular, and of the opulence of the culture it immortalizes.

In his accustomed self-effacing manner, Selvon broaches many concerns in his fiction, taken up much later by teachers, professional linguists and politicians. We can safely say that Selvon's brazen use of Trinidadian dialect gave welcome impetus to those who began to and still study the language of West Indians and compile dictionaries of island creoles (Allsopp, Le Page, Cassidy, Winer, among others). In his unabashed valorization of the vernacular, Selvon brings a long-overdue legitimacy to a linguistic register that has proved an invaluable tool in classrooms and to a variety of professionals. In his presentation of Indo-Trinidadian peasants and the Afro-Trinidadian working class, he invests both communities with a sense of pride and satisfaction in their separate struggles for self-actualization. In his advocacy of a meaningful understanding of creolization as a social ideal for Trinidad, Selvon anticipates the call of many politicians, intellectuals and calypsonians, who grasp the need for all citizens, to feel part of a multi-racial society without relinquishing their ethnic ties, rituals and values.

Undoubtedly, Selvon, had he lived, would feel a deep sense of pride in knowing that he predicted, even if vaguely, in his characterization of Tiger and Romesh that Trinidad one day would elect an Indo-Trinidadian prime minister (Basdeo Panday in 2001 and Kamla Persad-Bissessar in 2010). Additionally, he would feel equally proud to know that Tiger's inchoate artistic ambitions find their absolute fruition in Naipaul being awarded the Nobel prize for literature; teasingly, both have their humble beginnings in the heartland village of Chaguanas, and for both Queen's Royal College is seen as the place of knowledge. Of course, Tiger fantasizes about attending the college (most probably, too, this is the city college Romesh attends in 'Cane Is Bitter'). Naipaul attends Queen's Royal College and is awarded a scholarship to study in England; Romesh at the end of *The Plains of Caroni* is off to England on a company scholarship. Selvon's visionary presentation of the apotheosis of the Indo-Trinidadian peasant and of the Afro-Trinidadian working class individual (Moses of *The Lonely Londoners*), and his seminal use of the language of Trinidad make him the most democratic and predictive of writers. These achievements have not only made him one of the central figures in West Indian literature but also have made him a genuine literary pioneer. Notwithstanding the significant efforts of Alfred Mendes, Ralph de Boissière and C. L. R. James, among others, Selvon is the first to put his native land gloriously and indelibly on the literary map, totally fulfilling his primary objective. A genial, human acceptance and grasp of the common frailties and vast potential of West Indian man underpin his best narratives. In the struggle of his characters to overcome tremendous odds – historical, ethnic and personal – in their need to explore their creative urges and to become involved in politics, Selvon establishes, endorses, and lauds their heroic aspirations, as they seek to advance and transform society. So much and more make him an indispensable writer.

Notes

CHAPTER 1: POEMS

1. The vast majority of Selvon's poems were published in the *Trinidad Guardian*, whose archives (1917–80) were destroyed by fire in 1980. There is a microfilm copy of the *Trinidad Guardian* at the UWI Library, St Augustine, Trinidad; unfortunately, many words of the poems are badly faded and indecipherable. There are copies of the newspaper in the National Archives in Port of Spain, but copies of the *Sunday Weekly* (January 1947–May 1947), which accompanied the *Guardian*, are missing. The Selvon Collection at UWI, St Augustine, however, contains clear copies of many of the poems. All Selvon's poems, published and unpublished, are included in *The Poems of Sam Selvon*, edited and annotated by Roydon Salick (Royston, Herts.: Cane Arrow Press, 2012).
2. Selvon married Draupadi (Selvon spells it 'Droupadi') Persaud in 1947. She died of cancer in her native Guyana in 1972.

CHAPTER 2: RADIO DRAMAS

1. Both volumes are published by Peepal Tree Press (1998, 1991). In her introduction to *El Dorado West One*, Susheila Nasta explores the relationship between the seven-part drama and *The Lonely Londoners*. However, there is no attempt to assess the success or merits of the radio drama. No notes accompany the plays in *Highway in the Sun*.
2. Selvon also adapted many radio dramas from his short stories. Selvon's most entertaining radio drama is 'The Magic Stick' (aired on BBC Radio, 19 June 1971), his wonderfully comic adaptation of Ismith Khan's *The Obeah Man* (1964). In the novel, both Hop

and Drop and Massahood suffer ignominious deaths; in the drama, nobody dies, although a bleeding Massahood is taken to hospital. Zampi offers Hop and Drop a choice between the stick and the alluring Zolda. The cripple chooses the stick and invites everyone to 'play mas' and enjoy himself. Selvon's preference for the comic is again very clear in this drama.

3. Tim Crook, *Radio Drama: Theory and Practice* (London: Routledge, 1999), 157. This book is highly recommended.

CHAPTER 3: SHORT FICTION

1. Tate & Lyle, the British sugar conglomerate invited Selvon to write a book on Trinidad's sugar industry. Selvon completed *The Plains of Caroni* in 1969, while at Tacarigua, a village, like Barataria, that had a special appeal for him.

2. *Ways of Sunlight* (Harlow: Longman, 1957); *Foreday Morning: Selected Prose 1946–86*, ed. and intro. Kenneth Ramchand & Shusheila Nasta (Harlow: Longman, 1989). *Foreday Morning* contains non-fictional pieces, an excerpt from an untitled novel in progress (1986) and Selvon's address on growing up as a creolized Indo-Trinidadian. For this collection, Ramchand wrote the introduction and Nasta compiled the bibliography.

3. To categorize Selvon short pieces according to style is to divide them into three groups: dialect, standard and hybrid. The dialect pieces are written wholly in dialect; this is a large group that comprises all the London-based ballads and a few of the urban narratives. The standard pieces employ Standard English as the language of narration, description and dialogue. These form a surprisingly large group and includes the first six stories that Selvon wrote; indeed, only two of the first fifteen pieces are not standard. As late as 1982, Selvon returned to the standard narrative: in 'Ralphie at the Races' the two protagonists, Ralphie, a recent 'immigrant from tropical Trinidad' and Angus, 'a fellow Trinidadian, who had been living in Calgary for seven years' speak, except for one or two brief lapses, Standard English. The third group employs a mixture of Standard English and dialect: standard for narration and description and dialect for conversation. Selvon's short fiction is divided almost equally among these three categories. Of course, such a categorization tells nothing of theme, setting and characterization.

4. Although in 2011, Trinidad & Tobago is more racially mixed than it was some sixty years ago, it remains an island in which place

of residence and nomenclature are fairly safe indicators of ethnicity. For example, Prakash Harripersad from Penal is almost certainly an Indo-Trinidadian, while Duncan Hinds from Morvant is almost certainly an Afro-Trinidadian. If Prakash Harripersad were from Morvant, Trinidadians would assume because of his name that he is an Indo-Trinidadian. The ethnic equation is complicated by the fact that such surnames as Martin, Paul, Joseph and John, among others, are used by both Afro-Trinidadians and Indo-Trinidadians.

5. In this letter to Sir George Beaumont (8 April 1808), Wordsworth speaks of the blessing that derives from 'habits of exalted imagination'. *The Letters of Dorothy and William Wordsworth, The Middle Years (1806–11)*, vol. II, ed. Ernest de Selincourt, rev. Mary Moorman (Oxford: Clarendon Press, 1969), 209–11.

6. For a fuller discussion of the relationship among the three versions of the Johnson-and-the-cascadura narrative, see my chapter, 'Those Who Eat the Cascadura', *The Novels of Samuel Selvon: A Critical Study* (Connecticut: Greenwood Press, 2001), 59–73.

CHAPTER 4: NOVELS

1. More detailed analyses of the ten novels are contained in my first book on Selvon, *The Novels of Samuel Selvon: A Critical Study*.

2. It is hard to understand why Selvon uses the homophonic 'salmon' since as early as 1949, he uses one of the two accepted spellings, 'The poor and destitute find some solace here, in the shade of the spreading samaan tree . . .' ('The Same Old Life' *FM* 46). The saman, long naturalized in Trinidad, because of its size, height and patulousness, is commonly found in parks and large private properties. It creates its own micro-ecosystem housing many species of birds, iguanas, spiders, tree frogs, native orchids, lianas and other epiphytes. Such a tree Selvon describes in *TWEC* (55).

3. 'Poya' is the most common term employed by Indo-Trinidadians peasants to describe the tool used by cane-cutters. It is not a Bhojpuri word, but a nasalized approximation of 'poniard' (dagger), a word in use in Trinidad long before indenture. Two types of 'poya' were available to the cane-cutter: a straight-blade cutlass (Balgobin's), and one with a blade bent at angle that allowed the bent portion to rest flat on the ground (commonly called 'swiper' and 'brushing cutlass'). 'Fork', another vital

implement, was also given a heavy nasalization by Indo-Trinidadian peasants. Even though rural Indo-Trinidadians still use 'poya', cutlass (sometimes 'cutlash') is the word most ubiquitously used for the cutting implement. Selvon does not exaggerate the inseparability of man and his 'poya'. Negatively, it has had a long history of violence, social and domestic, among this ethnic group, so much so that it is the one implement most readily associated with lower-class Indo-Trinidadians – 'The Indians had a casual way of swinging a cutlass to level things out . . .' (*TWEC* 95).

4. With its focus on finding a home for West Indians, *HL* may be read as Selvon's comment on and hope for Federation, an abortive but significant excursion in regional history, in which he took a keen interest, evidenced in his poem 'Federation' (1949).

5. It is heartening to know that 'lime' (perhaps the most distinctive Trinidadianism) has found a place in the *New Shorter Oxford English Dictionary* (1996) though it has been omitted from the eleventh edition of the *Concise Oxford English Dictionary* (2008). Like other crucial words, 'lime' has metamorphosed from being an aimless street activity to an event occurring anywhere (beach, river, bar, house, etc) that demands preparation, planning, and management. Cooking, drinking and 'old talk' are staple activities of a 'lime'. What 'the boys' create in Moses's basement room in *The Lonely Londoners* is essentially a 'lime'; the excursion and activities on the banks of the Thames near Hampton Court in *The Housing Lark* comprise another version of the Trinidad 'lime.'

Selected Bibliography

WORKS BY SAMUEL SELVON

Novels

A Brighter Sun (London: Allan Wingate, 1952; London: Longman, 1989).

An Island is a World (London: Allan Wingate, 1955; Toronto: TSAR, 1993).

The Lonely Londoners (London: Allan Wingate, 1956; London: Longman, 1972; Toronto: TSAR, 1991).

Turn Again Tiger (London: MacGibbon & Kee, 1958; London: Heinemann, 1979).

I Hear Thunder (London: MacGibbon & Kee, 1963).

The Housing Lark (London: MacGibbon & Kee, 1965; Washington, D.,C.: Three Continents Press, 1990).

The Plains of Caroni (London: MacGibbon & Kee, 1970; Toronto: Williams-Wallace, 1986).

Those Who Eat the Cascadura (London: Davis-Poynter, 1972; Toronto: TSAR, 1990).

Moses Ascending (London: Davis-Poynter, 1975; London: Heinemann, 1984).

Moses Migrating (London: Longman, 1983; Washington, D.C.: Three Continents Press, 1992).

Short fiction

Ways of Sunlight (London: MacGibbon & Kee, 1957; London: Longman, 1973).

Foreday Morning. Compiled and introduced by Kenneth Ramchand and Susheila Nasta (London: Longman, 1989).

Radio dramas

El Dorado West One. Introduction by Susheila Nasta (Leeds: Peepal Tree Press, 1988).
Highway in the Sun (Leeds: Peepal Tree Press, 1991).

Poems

Trinidad Guardian. 15 December 1946; 12 January 1947; 26 January 1947; 2 February 1947; 9 February 1947; 16 February 1947; 2 March 1947; 23 March 1947; 13 April 1947; 20 April 1947; 11 May 1947; 25 May 1947; 1 June 1947; 20 July 1947; 24 July 1947; 14 September 1947; 7 December 1947; 18 January 1948; 29 February 1948; 11 July 1948; 8 August 1948; 14 November 1948; 3 July 1949; 25 September 1949.
BIM. III, 2, (1949), 249; V, 20, (1954), 299).
Caribbean Voices: An Anthology of West Indian Poetry, ed. John Figueroa (London: Evans Bros, 1971, 160–4).
Savacou, 7/8 (1973), 25.
The Poems of Sam Selvon, edited by Roydon Salick (Royston, Herts.: Cane Arrow Press, 2012).

Selected interviews

Dasenbrook, Reed and Feroza Jussawalla, 'Interview with Sam Selvon', *Tiger's Triumph: Celebrating Sam Selvon.* ed. Susheila Nasta & Anna Rutherford (London: Dangaroo Press, 1995) 114–25.
Durix, Jean-Pierre, 'Talking of *Moses Ascending* with Samuel Selvon', *Commonwealth: Essays and Studies*, 10: 2 (Spring 1988), 11–13.
Fabre, Michel, 'Samuel Selvon: Interviews and Conversations', *Critical Perspectives on Sam Selvon.* ed. Susheila Nasta (Washington, D.C.: Three Continents Press, 1988), 64–76.
Nasta, Shusheila, 'The Moses Trilogy: Sam Selvon Discusses His London Novels', *Wasafiri*, 1: 2 (1986), 5–10.
Nazareth, Peter, 'Interview with Sam Selvon', *Critical Perspectives on Sam Selvon*, ed. Susheila Nasta (Washington, D.C.: Three Continents Press, 1988) 95–103.
Ramchand, Kenneth, 'Sam Selvon Talking: A Conversation with Kenneth Ramchand', *Critical Perspectives on Sam Selvon* ed. Susheila Nasta (Washington, D.C.: Three Continents Press, 1988) 95–103.
Roberts, Kevin and Andra Thakur, 'Christened with Snow: A Conversation with Sam Selvon', *Ariel*, 27: 2 (April 1996), 89–115.
Wyke, Clement, 'Interview with Samuel Selvon', *Chimo* (Spring 1981), 30–8.

CRITICAL STUDIES

Ball, John Clement, *Imagining London: Postcolonial Fiction and the Transnational Metropolis* (Toronto: University of Toronto Press, 2004).

Barratt, Harold, 'An Island Is Not a World: A Reading of Sam Selvon's *An Island Is A World*' *ARIEL* 27: 2 (April 1996), 25–34.

———, 'Dialect, Maturity, and the Land in Sam Selvon's *A Brighter Sun*: A Reply', *English Studies In Canada* 8: 3 (1981), 329–37.

———, 'From Colony to Colony: Selvon's Expatriate West Indians' in *Perspectives on Sam Selvon*, edited and compiled by Susheila Nasta (Washington, D.C.: Three Continents Press, 1988), 250–9.

———, 'Sam Selvon's Tiger: In Search of Self-Awareness', *Reworlding: The Literature of the Indian Diaspora*, ed. Emmanuel S. Nelson (Connecticut: Greenwood Press, 1992), 105–14.

———, 'Individual Integrity in Selvon's *Turn Again Tiger* and *Those Who Eat The Cascadura*', *The Toronto South Asian Review*, vol. 5, no. 1 (Summer 1986), 153–9.

Baugh, Edward, 'Exiles, Guerillas and Visions of Eden', *Queen's Quarterly* 84 (1977), 273–86).

———, 'Friday in Crusoe's City: The Question of Language in Two West Indian Novels of Exile', *ACLALS*, 5th Ser. 3 (1980), 1–12.

Birbalsingh, Frank, 'Samuel Selvon and the West Indian Renaissance', *ARIEL* 8 (1977), 5–22).

Brathwaite, Edward, 'Sir Galahad and the Islands', *BIM* 7 (July–December 1957), 8–16.

Brown, Wayne, '"A Greatness and a Vastness": The Search for God in the Fiction of Sam Selvon', *ARIEL* 27: 2 (April 1996), 35–46.

Clarke, Austin, *Passage Back Home: A Personal Reminiscence of Sam Selvon* (Toronto: Exile Press, 2004).

Dasenbrook, Reed, & Feroza, Jussawala, 'Interview with Sam Selvon', *Tiger's Triumph:. Celebrating Sam Selvon*, ed. Susheila Nasta & Anna Rutherford (London: Dangaroo Press, 1995, 114–25).

Dawson, Ashley, *Mongrel Nation: Diasporic Culture and the Making of Postcolonial Britain* (Ann Arbor: University of Michigan Press, 2007).

Dyer, Rebecca, 'Immigration, Postwar London, and the Politics of Everyday Living in Sam Selvon's Fiction', *Cultural Critique* 52 (Fall 2002), 108–44.

Fabre, Michel, 'Interview with Sam Selvon', *Perspectives on Sam Selvon*, edited and compiled by Susheila Nasta (Washington, D.C.: Three Continents Press, 1988), 64–76.

———, 'Samuel Selvon', *West Indian Literature*, ed. Bruce King (London: Macmillan, 1979), 111–25.

——, 'From Trinidad to London: Tone and Language in Samuel Selvon's Novels', *The Literary Half-Yearly* 20 (January 1979), 71–80.

——, 'The Queen's Calypso: Linguistic and Narrative Strategies in the Fiction of Samuel Selvon', *Caribbean Essays and Studies* 3 (1977–8), 69–76.

Forbes, Curdella, *From Nation to Diaspora: Samuel Selvon, George Lamming and the Cultural Performance of Gender* (Kingston: UWI Press, 2005).

Gikandi, Simon, *Writing in Limbo; Modernism in Caribbean Literature* (Ithaca: Cornell University Press, 1992).

Joseph, Margaret Paul, *Caliban in Exile: The Outsider in Caribbean Fiction* (Connecticut: Greenwood Press, 1992).

Khan, Ismith, *The Jumbie Bird* (London: MacGibbon & Kee, 1961).

——, *The Obeah Man* (Toronto: TSAR, 1995).

——, 'Remembering Sammy', *Tiger's Triumph: Celebrating Sam Selvon*, ed. by Susheila Nasta and Anna Rutherford (London: Dangaroo Press, 1995), 1–13.

Looker, Mark, *Atlantic Passages: History, Community and Language in the Fiction of Sam Selvon* (New York: Peter Lang, 1996).

McLeod, John, *Postcolonial London* (London: Routledge, 2004).

Morris, Mervyn, 'Introduction', *Moses Ascending* (London: Heinemann, 1984).

Naipaul, V.S., 'Caribbean Voices – An Island Is A World', *Perspectives on Sam Selvon*, edited and compiled Susheila Nasta (Washington, D.C.: Three Continents Press, 1988), 112.

Nasta, Susheila, edited and compiled, *Perspectives on Sam Selvon* (Washington D.C.: Three Continents Press, 1988).

——, 'Samuel Selvon: Prolific! Popular!' (Afterword), *Moses Migrating* (Washington, D.C.: Three Continents Press, 1992).

——, 'Setting Up Home in a City of Words: Sam Selvon's London Novels', *Tiger's Triumph: Celebrating Sam Selvon*, edited Susheila Nasta and Anna Rutherford (London: Dangaroo Press, 1995), 78–95.

—— and Anna Rutherford, *Tiger's Triumph: Celebrating Sam Selvon* (London: Dangaroo Press, 1995).

Nazareth, Peter, 'The Clown in the Slave Ship', *Perspectives on Sam Selvon*, ed. Susheila Nasta (Washington, D.C.: Three Continents Press, 1988), 234–9.

——, 'Interview with Sam Selvon', *World Literature Written in English* 18: 2 (1979), 420–37.

Okereke, Grace Eche, 'Samuel Selvon's Evolution from *A Brighter Sun* to *Turn Again Tiger*: An Expansion of Vision and a Development of Form', *Tiger's Triumph: Celebrating Sam Selvon*, ed. Susheila Nasta and Anna Rutherford (London: Dangaroo Press, 1995), 35–50.

Pouchet Paquet, Sandra, 'Introduction', *Turn Again Tiger* (London: Heinemann, 1979).

Procter, James, *Dwelling Places: Postwar Black British Writing* (Manchester: University of Manchester Press, 2003).

Ramchand, Kenneth, 'Comedy as Evasion in the Later Novels of Sam Selvon', *Something Rich and Strange: Selected Essays on Sam Selvon*, edited and introduced Martin Zehnder (Leeds: Peepal Tree Press, 2003), 85–106.

——, *An Introduction to the Study of West Indian Literature* (London: Thomas Nelson, 1976).

——, 'Song of Innocence, Song of Experience: Sam Selvon's *The Lonely Londoners* as a Literary Work', *World Literature Written in English* 21 (1982), 644–54.

——, 'The Love Songs of Samuel Dickson Selvon', *ARIEL* 27: 2 (April 1996), 77–88.

Ramraj, Victor, 'The Philosophy of Neutrality: The Treatment of Political Militancy in Samuel Selvon's *Moses Ascending* and *Moses Migrating*', *Literature and Commitment*, ed. G. Sharma (Toronto: TSAR, 1988), 109–15.

——, 'Selvon's Londoners: From Centre to Periphery', *Language and Literature*, ed. Satendra Nanan, *ACLALS* (1980), 297–306.

Rohlehr, Gordon, 'The Folk in Caribbean Literature', *Perspectives on Sam Selvon*, edited and compiled Susheila Nasta (Washington, D.C.: Three Continents Press, 1988), 29–43.

Salick, Roydon, *The Novels of Samuel Selvon: A Critical Study* (Connecticut: Greenwood Press, 2001).

Sandhu, Sukdev, *London Calling: How Black and Asian Writers Imagined a City* (London: Harper Collins, 2003).

Sindoni, Maria Grazia, *Creolizing Culture: A Study on Sam Selvon's Work* (New Delhi: Atlantic Publishers, 2006).

Tiffin, Helen, '"Under the Kiff-Kiff Laughter": Stereotype and Subversion in Moses Ascending and Moses Migrating', *Tiger's Triumph: Celebrating Sam Selvon*, ed. Susheila Nasta and Anna Rutherford (London: Dangaroo Press, 1995), 130–9).

Warner-Lewis, Maureen, 'Samuel Selvon's Linguistic Extravaganza: *Moses Ascending*', *Caribbean Quarterly* 28 (December 1982), 60–9.

Wyke, Clement, *Sam Selvon's Dialectical Style and Fictional Strategy* (Vancouver: University of British Columbia Press, 1991).

——, 'Voice and Identity in Sam Selvon's Late Short Fiction', *ARIEL* 27; 2 (April 1996), 133–47.

Zehnder, Martin, edited and introduced, *Something Rich and Strange: Selected Essays on Sam Selvon* (Leeds: Peepal Tree Press, 2003).

Index